T0311604

Cambridge Elements ≡

Elements in Political Economy
edited by
David Stasavage
New York University

GEOGRAPHY, CAPACITY, AND INEQUALITY

Volume I: Spatial Inequality

Pablo Beramendi
Duke University

Melissa Rogers
Claremont Graduate University

CAMBRIDGE
UNIVERSITY PRESS

University Printing House, Cambridge CB2 8BS, United Kingdom

One Liberty Plaza, 20th Floor, New York, NY 10006, USA

477 Williamstown Road, Port Melbourne, VIC 3207, Australia

314–321, 3rd Floor, Plot 3, Splendor Forum, Jasola District Centre,
New Delhi – 110025, India

103 Penang Road, #05–06/07, Visioncrest Commercial, Singapore 238467

Cambridge University Press is part of the University of Cambridge.

It furthers the University's mission by disseminating knowledge in the pursuit of
education, learning, and research at the highest international levels of excellence.

www.cambridge.org
Information on this title: www.cambridge.org/9781108828406
DOI: 10.1017/9781108908702

© Pablo Beramendi and Melissa Rogers 2022

First published 2022

A catalogue record for this publication is available from the British Library.

ISBN 978-1-108-82840-6 Paperback
ISSN 2398-4031 (online)
ISSN 2514-3816 (print)

Geography, Capacity, and Inequality

Volume I: Spatial Inequality
Elements in Political Economy

DOI: 10.1017/9781108908702
First published online: April 2022

Pablo Beramendi
Duke University

Melissa Rogers
Claremont Graduate University

Author for correspondence: Pablo Beramendi, pb45@duke.edu

Abstract: In this Element, we investigate how economic geography, the distribution of subnational economic endowments within a nation, shapes long-run patterns of inequality through its impact on the development of fiscal capacity. We present an argument that links economic geography to capacity through different types of industrialization processes. We show how early industrializers shape spatial distributions domestically by investing in productivity across their nations, and externally by reinforcing spatial polarization among late industrializers. We also show how differences in economic geography impact the process of capacity building, setting the stage for the modern politics of redistribution discussed in Volume II. We support this argument with descriptive data, case studies, and cross-national analyses.

Keywords: economic geography, industrialization, state capacity, inequality, redistribution

ISBNs: 9781108828406 (PB), 9781108908702 (OC)
ISSNs: 2398-4031 (online), 2514-3816 (print)

Contents

1 Geography, Industrialization, and Capacity: An Overview

The history of political development suggests that a functioning, capable state is a necessary condition for the political pursuit of equality (Besley and Persson, 2011; Soifer, 2013). Both the regulation of markets and the reallocation of income and wealth through the political process requires the capacity to measure, count, record, tax, and distribute. A capable state does not guarantee effective regulation or redistribution, but without one neither is possible. Fiscal capacity is the ability of governments to extract sufficient levels of revenue to fund policy goals. It poses a constraint on those who lack it but does not determine the choices of those who have it.

Conceptually, it is important to distinguish between capacity and policy choice. Effective taxation and redistribution can occur only if (1) effective state bureaucracies are fully in place, (2) those bureaucracies have developed to have relatively similar levels of capacity, and (3) there is enough political support within the polity to enact such interventions. Capacity refers to the potential to implement effectively a political choice: it requires resources, organization, and personnel (Dincecco, 2017).

In the two volumes that compose this Element we highlight the importance of spatial inequalities (both economic and political) to the development of fiscal capacity. We argue that differential capacity levels are a key driver of the politics of inequality around the globe today because capacity serves as the link between legacies of spatial inequalities and variation in levels of redistribution. In Figure 1 we provide an overview of the focal variables in our analysis: the link between spatial inequality (measured with the coefficient of variation in subnational GDP per capita) and fiscal capacity (measured with total tax revenue as a percentage of GDP) in Figure 1(a), and the link between fiscal capacity and redistribution (measured with the reduction in the Gini coefficient through government taxes and transfers) in Figure 1(b). In Figure 1(a), we see a strong negative correlation between subnational disparities in economic productivity and long-run fiscal capacity. In Figure 1(b), we see that this fiscal capacity is, in turn, a strong predictor of redistributive effort. Countries with high levels of tax collection are those that make the greatest efforts to reduce inequality. They are also the ones with less skewed economic geographies.

Within nearly all countries of the world, there is an enormous spatial skew in prosperity, as certain regions and cities pull far ahead of the rest of their nations. Concentration of economic advantage, in turn, translates into political influence. The spatial skew in economic fortunes reflects the combined effect of geographic endowments and industrialization processes. Because of specific characteristics of their process of economic modernization, early industrializers

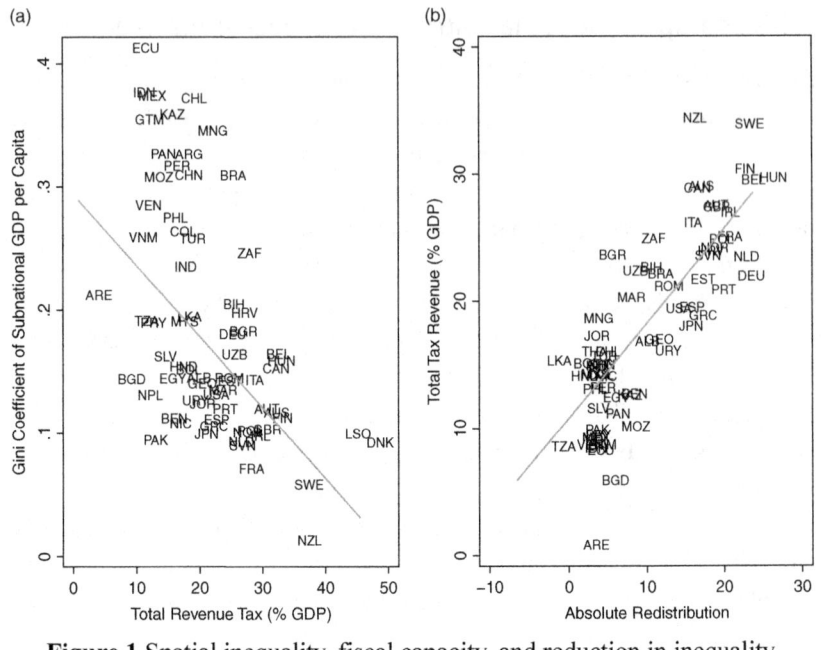

Figure 1 Spatial inequality, fiscal capacity, and reduction in inequality.

Cross-sectional data of national mean values. (a) Correlation is p = −0.54. Independent variable: Gini coefficient of subnational GDP per capita (Rogers, 2015). Dependent variable: Total Tax Revenue (% GDP) (Prichard et al., 2014). (b) The correlation is p = 0.63. Independent variable: Total Tax Revenue (% GDP) (Prichard et al., 2014). Dependent variable: Absolute Redistribution (Gini Market-Gini Disposable) (Solt, 2009).

conquered space both internally by developing integrated national markets, and externally by conditioning the economic and political institutions of dependent territories of those areas that eventually became late industrializers. In contrast, the industrialization process in late industrializers was largely subsidiary to the export of agricultural commodities, which limited investments in large-scale industrialization and consolidated skewed spatial distributions over time.[1]

---

[1] We follow Bentzen et al. (2013) in identifying industrialization as the point at which nonagricultural employment surpasses agricultural employment. We place the distinction of early versus late at 1950. "Late" and "early" industrialization are relative designations. For example, much has been written about France's delayed industrialization in comparison to the United Kingdom or Germany (Allen, 2009). Similarly, Sweden is considered a late industrializer on the European continent, but certainly is not in the global perspective. On the other hand, we have designated Finland a late developer according to this schema, with its long-term success attributable to its relative uniform geography and global position. We intend for the timing of industrialization to represent important factors about the nature of the global economy, the global political system, and the characteristics of most countries that industrialized later or not at all. Thus we emphasize that the early versus late distinction is stylized. We include a list of early and late industrializing nations in Appendix 1.2.

To analyze these links between different types of industrialization and spatial concentrations of economic and political advantage, we adopt a long-run view and analyze relationships between the patterns of industrialization, economic geography, and the state's capacity to redistribute. We show three things.

First, natural economic endowments are highly linked to spatial inequalities in late industrializers but largely decoupled in early industrializing nations. The transformation of spatial inequalities over time diverged in early and late industrializing nations. In early industrializers, the process of industrialization and its aftermath reduced spatial inequalities. This reflects the physical and economic integration of previously peripheral areas in early industrializers into the national economy. In late industrializers, by contrast, spatial inequalities were exacerbated, making them spike beyond their already high levels. The incorporation of the periphery in late developers was in all cases incomplete, and often peripheral areas were left behind as the central cities grew more affluent and diversified. Differences in spatial inequalities persist to the present, even if these nations' cities, through agglomeration and innovation, become drivers of development (Glaeser, 2011).

Second, we establish the connection between spatial inequalities and cross-national differences in fiscal capacity. Through a variety of political mechanisms, more skewed distributions constrained both capacity and, ultimately, the ability to curb different forms of inequality via redistributive politics. Marshalling a plethora of indicators on capacity and a large number of specifications, we show that an uneven economic geography is a strong predictor of lower levels of capacity, particularly among late industrializers. Early industrializers develop through the internal and external conquest of space. Internally, national markets are integrated via infrastructural investments. Externally, colonial expansion facilitates access to commodities and broadens the scope of markets. Crucially, the external conquest of space, via colonial rule, reinforces the spatial economic and political polarization among would-be late industrializers.

Third, capacity operates as an endogenous mechanism through which early patterns of concentration of economic and political advantage shape the ability to redistribute today. The combination of economic geography and colonial rule conditions early capacity investments. Moreover, geopolitical factors reinforce the initial divergence in capacity stocks. The competition, via interstate wars, for additional sources of commodities and demand among early industrializers further enhances the gap in fiscal state development relative to late industrializers. As a result of these processes, polities at different levels of development confront structural transformations from fundamentally divergent capacity levels. Late industrializers face their integration into the international economy or their transition into the digital era from a much weaker position. Their ability to equalize fortunes across classes or regions is more limited, thus shaping both interpersonal and spatial inequalities in current times.

Our analysis of the relationship between geography, capacity, and inequality proceeds in two steps: Volume I focuses on the origins of spatial inequalities and their impact on capacity development. Volume II focuses on the implications these differences in capacity have for the politics of redistribution to address interpersonal and spatial inequalities. Jointly, these two volumes provide a new perspective to understand why and how differences in capacity level anchor countries' ability to cope with rising inequalities today. Our efforts speak to several lines of research in political economy.

Through the connection between space and capacity, we revisit an old theme in comparative development going back to Gerschenkron's (1962) idea that "in several, very important respects, the development of a backward country may, by the very virtue of its backwardness, tend to differ fundamentally from that of an advanced country" (p. 6). He pointed to the differential role of credit institutions and their relation to the state, to ideology, and to the survival of serfdom as relevant factors, among others, to understand heterogeneous trajectories in European industrialization. Here we expand the scope of his fundamental intuition to better understand how spatial differences in the way that economic geography shaped state formation determined capacity to meet rising social and economic demands. For early industrializers, concentrated mainly in Western Europe, North America, and Australia, the fundamental dilemma is how to adapt relatively strong fiscal states and public services to structural changes and growing demands. For late industrializers, concentrated mainly in Latin America, Africa, and parts of Asia, the challenge is how to cope with the growing importance of manufactures in an increasingly integrated market for consumables with much weaker fiscal states and public services. We contend that these differences in capacity are essential to understand the political economy of inequality and its dynamics across the world.

Our approach also connects with research highlighting the global division of labor as a critical barrier to economic prosperity in late industrializing nations. In dependency theory, the early industrializers set up an unfair system of exchange controlled by themselves, in which late industrializing nations supply (at exploitative prices) the lower-value inputs that fuel the higher-value finished goods produced in early industrializing nations (Cardoso and Faletto, 1979). By relegating late industrializers to providers of inputs to the industrialization process, the timing of a nation's industrialization likely shaped the spatial distribution of economic productivity. The majority of materials exported from the late industrializers to the early industrializers were primary commodities (whether raw or partially processed goods), which reinforced the advantage of those parts of the nation with good natural economic endowments (Haber, 2005). In this way, the global system of economic dependency exacerbated spatial inequalities in late industrializers, contributing to the political conflicts that undermine fiscal capacity development.

We speak to the literature on economic geography and developmental outcomes. We build on previous research that sees geography and institutions not as mutually exclusive explanations of developmental and distributive outcomes, but rather complements in the explanation of inequality patterns (Diamond, 2013). This literature has focused on the relationship between economic geography and various mechanisms behind the prosperity of nations: property rights (Acemoglu and Johnson, 2005; Acemoglu et al., 2001), inequality and human capital (Engerman and Sokoloff, 2002; Galor et al., 2009; Nunn, 2008; Sokoloff and Engerman, 2000), forms of production (Dell, 2010), legal traditions (Besley and Persson, 2011), and political competition (Berkowitz and Clay, 2011). Somewhat surprisingly, much less attention has been paid to the connection between geography and the strength of fiscal institutions (Boone, 2003) and how this in turn helps explain today's patterns of inequality. In our view, a better understanding of the connection between economic geography and capacity will illuminate important mechanisms behind the structural inequalities that constrain development in the long run (Easterly, 2007). In particular, a focus on the spatial concentration of economic and political influence helps to explain why in some countries, mostly early industrializers, legal and fiscal capacity grow and reinforce each other, whereas in others, mostly late industrializers, there emerges a decoupling of the rule of law and the fiscal strength of public institutions (Besley and Persson, 2009).

We also provide a new perspective on how international and domestic factors interact to shape both capacity and inequality around the world. Recent contributions have shown major international conflicts to be an important factor behind the state's fiscal expansion (Boix, 2015; Dincecco, 2011; Queralt, 2019; Scheve and Stasavage, 2010; Tilly, 1992). Our argument does not seek to pit domestic versus international factors in a sort of artificial (and analytically rather absurd) race. Wars, in our account, by affecting mainly early industrializers, are critical events that shape the global geography of capacity asymmetrically. They are structural breaks that work to reinforce preexisting patterns of capacity divergence. Relative to existing bellicist capacity arguments, we pay special attention to economic geography as setting the playing field. Relative to existing geography-based theories, we highlight the long-run legacy of industrialization and its impact through changes in the composition and evolution of political elites.

Finally, by studying the conditions leading to underinvestment in capacity, we also speak to a recent literature on how different legacies of political and economic modernization shape efficiency and distributional outcomes today (Albertus and Menaldo, 2014; Kurtz, 2013; Soifer, 2015). A central idea in the pages that follow concerns the corrosive nature of inequality: some dimensions of inequality undermine the ability of democracy to control inequality itself. One of the key mechanisms in this recursive process is the consolidation of different capacity legacies over time. This, in turn, speaks to a broader debate about the contextual effects of institutional and capacity reforms (Hanson, 2014, 2015; Soifer, 2013) and in particular, to recent debates about the conditions under which democracy and inequality can coexist.

2 The Argument: Industrialization, Geography, and Capacity

The central argument of this Element is that the spatial concentration of economic (and political) power constrained the development of state capacity in many parts of the world. It did so by conditioning elites' preferences for investments in the development of state institutions and their ability to carry these preferences through. These initial choices led to fundamental differences in capacity stocks that, in turn, anchored the way countries responded to subsequent structural transformations. In particular, initial capacity stocks shaped the size and progressivity of fiscal and public insurance systems, thus conditioning the evolution of different types of inequalities.

The link between geography and capacity is spatial in two ways. First, concentrated spatial economic endowments lead to distributive conflict, with elites from the most productive regions highly skeptical of central capacity that may be redistributed outward to peripheral regions. Second, there is a sequential hierarchy between early movers and the rest of the world. The success in building strong states in early industrializers allowed them to shape the social structure and early institutional investments in the developing world. Successes in developing capacity among early industrializers and early democratizers worked to actually constrain capacity development in late industrializers through the economic and institutional legacy of colonialism, which intensified spatial polarization across the developing world.

This polarization shaped elites' preferences about capacity investments and their ability to overcome the very constraints imposed by skewed economic geography. It did so by shaping how different countries prioritized investments at the time of industrialization and by leading to a fundamental divergence in capacity stocks across countries. This initial divergence was further reinforced by the incidence of international wars and their impact on fiscal development across countries. Early movers fought, among other reasons, to expand or retain their colonial rule, to maintain a grip on areas from which to transfer resources back to the metropole. These military conflicts, in turn, led to additional expansion and consolidation of effective state institutions among the early movers. In contrast, by the time colonies become independent, interstate war was no longer a major engine of state development. The initial spatial divergence derived from colonialism was only exacerbated by the link between war and capacity development. There is a world of metropoles engaged in wars, out of which strong states emerge, and a world of colonies in which interstate wars are either largely absent, or where war was not linked to strong state development. Fiscal bureaucracies grow strong in the former, feebly in the latter.

As a result, states with different trajectories in terms of capacity development faced structural transformations on very different footings. Early industrializers, mostly metropoles with a long history of war engagement, managed the expansion of manufacturing (and the full incorporation of labor and women into democratic politics) and the subsequent transition to the service economy through the provision of public goods and large public insurance systems. Despite significant heterogeneity, they managed to slow down the growth in interpersonal inequality for several decades (Boix, 2019; Iversen and Soskice, 2019). At the same time, spatial inequalities remained relatively low, again with some significant variation across cases (to which we return in Section 5). This was primarily possible because their large and moderately progressive fiscal systems generated enough revenue to meet the cost of these responses. By contrast, the nations of the periphery managed their late incorporation into the industrial world and the international economy on much weaker grounds. Their fiscal effort is consistently much smaller and regressive, ultimately unable to significantly reduce interpersonal inequalities beyond adjustments on the margin. Moreover, spatial inequalities only grew stronger, further undermining the feasibility of redistributive efforts over time. Low-capacity legacies nurture a self-enforcing dynamic between interpersonal and spatial inequalities.

In what follows, we develop this argument in detail. We begin by presenting the core premises in our analytical framework. We characterize the decision to initiate and expand industrialization (in production and spatial terms) as a calculation made by elites focused on maximization of returns on their assets. Second, we analyze the origin of different patterns of spatial concentration and how the latter conditioned elites' incentives and constraints in different waves of industrialization. Initial conditions are key to understanding investments and account for the early divergence in capacity stocks. The section ends with a summary of the main empirical implications following from our argument.

2.1 Analytical Framework: Premises

Fiscal capacity is an investment made by elites. It reflects both their decision to fund initiatives, such as military effort or the expansion of public goods, and the availability of alternative sources of revenue, such as natural resources or cheap credit. Public goods investments imply the adoption and generalization of technological innovations and a major effort on infrastructural development for the purpose of bolstering the economic productivity of a particular sector (or set thereof).

In line with a large literature on economic and political modernization, we assume there are two types of elites: agricultural elites A and capitalist elites C (Beramendi et al., 2018). Each type of elite has their sector-specific production skill: rural elites specialize in agricultural production, and capitalist elites in industrial production. y is the output per worker in its sector. The output per worker at the starting point for agricultural elites is y_A and that of capitalist elites is y_C.

Agricultural elites were typically the incumbent power-holders in society in the post-industrial period (Ansell and Samuels, 2014; Boix, 2003; Justman and Gradstein, 1999; Kuznets, 1955; Moore et al., 1993). In a proto-industrialization context, incumbent elites face three sequential decisions: first, whether to invest in a higher amount of public goods that may improve economic productivity; second, how to fund these public goods; and third, where in the nation to make those investments – throughout the nation, or in one or a small number of locations with comparative advantage in economic geography.

In theory, the nature of public good investments may work in favor of either elite. The implications of new public goods for the output of agricultural elites depends on how they affect the productivity of the agricultural sector relative to the industrial one. Greater industrial production may "crowd out" agricultural production (Rostow, 1959). In this case, agricultural elites stand to lose (or at least benefit less) from new public good investments, which will increase the pace at which the economy shifts from agriculture to industry (Congleton, 2010; Kaldor, 1963). Let λ reflect the "production cost" of crowding out to agricultural elites, where $0 < \lambda_A \leq 1$. Alternatively, new public good investments may actually enhance the overall productivity of the agricultural sector. In this case, let λ_A reflect the increasing returns accruing to agricultural elites, where $1 < \lambda_A$. Similarly, if $0 < \lambda_C \leq 1$, investments increase the production cost function of manufacturing to the benefit of agriculture. By contrast, if $\lambda_C > 1$, investments are generating increasing returns on the income of the rising industrial sector: the expansion of public goods investments makes each additional unit of investment generate a return higher than unity.

Regarding the organization of fiscal systems, we reason from three premises. First, we assume national and subnational borders as given.[2] Preindustrial taxation focused on land and tariffs (Mares and Queralt, 2015). We therefore make the assumption that tariffs will directly affect the level of pretax income of both actors, and that indirect taxes (such as tariffs) fall broadly on consumers. Thus, before industrialization, the income of agricultural elites is given by $y_A - T_L$, where T_L refers to taxes on land. The income of the incipient industrial elites remains y_C. Second, following Lindert (2004), Lizzeri and Persico (2004), Congleton (2010), Pincus and Robinson (2014), and Beramendi et al. (2018), we also assume that tax structures grow in complexity as a result of development. Taxes on land (T_L) or tariffs are no longer the fundamental pillars of revenue generation as fiscal structures become a more complex function of trade taxes (T_R), and ultimately, direct taxes on income (T_D), and indirect taxation (especially on consumption) (T_I). We define the combination of these three tax tools as T_{RDI}.

The expected postindustrial income for both agricultural and industrial elites is therefore given by, respectively, $Y_A^{\lambda A} - T_L - T_{DRI}$ and $Y_C^{\lambda C} - T_{RDI}$.

Accordingly, when deciding whether to undertake major public goods investments for the purpose of economic modernization and industrialization, elites face the following calculations:

- Agricultural elites will support the investment if $Y_A < Y_A^{\lambda A} - T_{RDI}$ and oppose it otherwise.
- Industrial elites will support the investment if $Y_C < Y_C^{\lambda C} - T_{RDI}$ and oppose it otherwise.
- Put differently, either elite will support investment *iff*:
  - $Y_A^{\lambda A} - y_A > T_{RDI}$ in the case of agricultural elites.
  - $Y_C^{\lambda C} - y_C > T_{RDI}$ in the case of industrial elites.

Figure 2 presents a summary of the possible strategies adopted by elites. Recall that if $\lambda_{A,C} \leq 1$, investments imply a relative increase in the cost of production in the given sector; by contrast, if $\lambda_{A,C} > 1$, investments trigger increasing returns and facilitate sectoral expansion.

---

[2] We know that borders are not strictly endogenous (Grossman and Lewis, 2014; Mazucca, 2017). This is an important area of future research at the intersection of political economy, distributive politics, and identity.

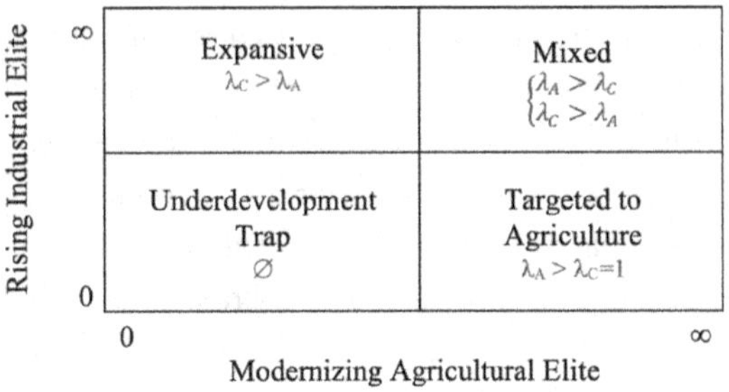

Rising Industrial Elite (vertical axis, from 0 to ∞)

	Modernizing Agricultural Elite →	
	Expansive $\lambda_C > \lambda_A$	Mixed $\begin{cases} \lambda_A > \lambda_C \\ \lambda_C > \lambda_A \end{cases}$
	Underdevelopment Trap $\varnothing$	Targeted to Agriculture $\lambda_A > \lambda_C = 1$

Figure 2 Investments in industrialization-oriented public goods.

Interestingly, this simple exercise captures a direct link between the nature of the multiplier effect of income among the different sectors and the level of taxes and fiscal capacity: unless the (expected) income effects associated with industrialization are sufficiently high, elites will support neither investments nor an increase in capacity to raise revenue to finance them.

This setup does not necessarily imply that agricultural and industrial elites are perpetually isolated from and competing with one another; indeed, we document considerable overlap in these groups in both early and late industrializers. What matters to our argument is the profile of investments ultimately adopted by elites. An industry-dominated portfolio of investment, for instance, does not require preexisting rural elites to be eliminated. As the initial competition resolves into a scenario in which the economic benefits of industrialization become apparent and increasingly prevalent, we expect old and new elites to merge over time in a process of class adaptation (Piketty, 2014). What matters is that the portfolio of investments is industry dominated (Ansell and Samuels, 2014). Similarly, agricultural dominated investment may coexist with intra-elite splits among rural producers or with partial investments in industry or relationships with foreign finance, often socially cemented as well. Our focus is on the dominant sector and its link to the investment-capacity portfolio.

The next hurdle is to analyze the specific conditions under which elites pursue the strategies summarized in Figure 2 and the implications of such strategies for the politics of capacity development and its connection to spatial inequalities.

2.2 The Roots of Capacity Divergence: Space and Industrialization

What governs the circumstances elites face when confronted with the choice of what and where to invest (i.e., the balance between λ_A and λ_C)? Part of the

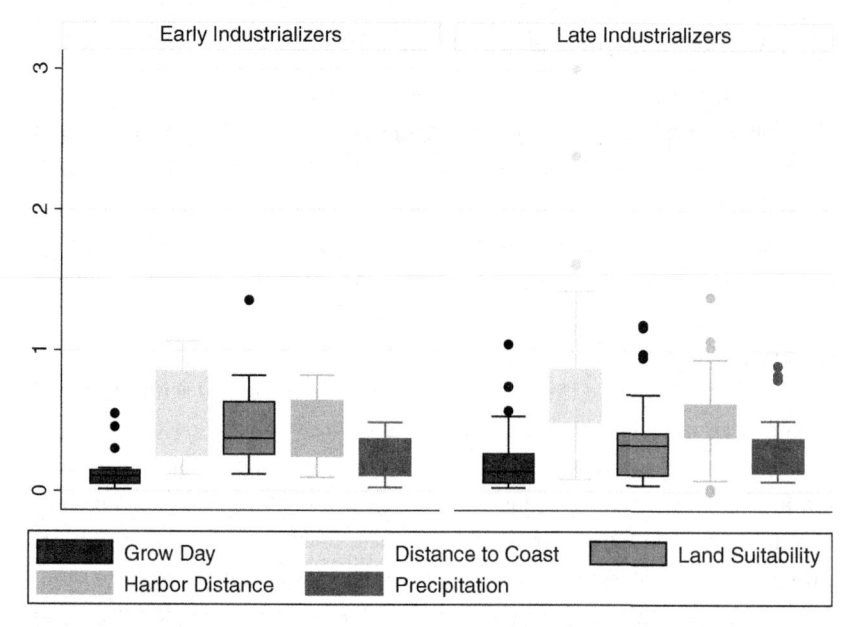

Figure 3 Spatial variation in subnational endowments, by industrialization timing.

answer lies in physical geography: rain, temperature, and humidity along with the quality of soil guide the type of production, the structure of land ownership, the nature of social hierarchies, and ultimately elites' preferences to change institutions or pursue different types of investments (Engerman and Sokoloff, 2002). Some versions of this logic see physical geography as a strict constraint (Dell et al., 2012; Diamond, 2013; Sachs, 2001).

Figure 3 shows the distribution of several measures of physical geography and land suitability across early and late industrializers. While it is clear that late industrializers have more variance within them, given their larger number, they are not on average different from their early industrializing counterparts with regard to subnational variation in physical geography. Physical geography is not a deterministic factor in the fate of countries. Nor is it an irrelevant one.

Others see geography as an exogenous condition that needs to be analyzed in combination with other phenomena, most prominently colonial legacies (Acemoglu and Robinson, 2006b; Easterly, 2007; Nugent and Robinson, 2010). Our analysis of the role of economic geography in the politics of capacity building joins in these efforts and pays attention to a relatively understudied causal channel: the interaction between economic geography and the spatial consequences of different waves of industrialization.

2.3 Early Movers and the Internal Conquest of Space

Economic historians situate the birthplace of industrialization in places where, for a variety of historical reasons, agricultural labor costs are high and there is access to low-cost energy sources, mostly coal (Allen, 2009; Allen et al., 2012; Barro, 1988).[3] These conditions nurture demand for technological innovation.[4] When this demand meets policy supply whereby property rights are protected and the system of representation facilitates the influence of parties supporting the expansion of public goods, increasing returns to industrial expansion accelerate ($\lambda_C > 1$).

Following Krugman (1991), increasing returns associated with locational proximity in manufacturing emerge thanks to the combination of three factors: labor pooling, technological spillovers across developing industries within the same sector (in this case, emerging manufacturers), and information sharing. For the combination of these factors to be successful, the growing production associated with new industries (often born out of "random" technological breakthroughs) must also have enough demand. That is, there must be a sufficiently large pool of potential consumers of the goods being produced, domestically or internationally, or both. The creation of a national market of consumers requires the formation of a transportation network for distribution. Moreover, as industrialization begins, rural workers move to where they expect to have better economic opportunities, thus decapitalizing agricultural production. Developing a network that permeates as much of the nation's territory as possible becomes the way of incorporating into the same system of exchange and allocating a large pool of consumers and workers. In turn, the ability to export requires manufactures to be easily portable to major points of distribution, which at the time of the first waves of industrialization are almost exclusively maritime ports.

Provided that these structural conditions increased the demand for technological innovations, industrial elites had therefore many reasons to invest large amounts of resources in the development of a well-integrated network for the transportation and distribution of goods, the circulation of energy, and the mobility of workers (Fremdling, 1977). These decisions have two direct consequences: first, they shape the spatial distribution of public goods

---

[3]   Relatively higher labor costs, in turn, reflect limited coercion and available exit options for workers (Acemoglu and Wolitzky, 2011).

[4]   Absent these conditions and absent, as well, the prospect of a large market to place output, there is no demand for technological innovation or public investments of any kind and the domestic economy remains stuck in a preindustrial equilibrium. The bottom-left cell in Figure 2 captures a situation in which investments in both sectors are virtually nonexistent.

investments; second, they require an attendant increase in revenue generation capacity, which is politically contentious as old and rising elites have divergent preferences about how to fund public expenditures.

Early industrializers distributed their investments spatially to maximize gains from natural features and in response to natural limitations on food production. Cities in early industrializers needed access to a nearby food supply for workers. The supply of food was limited by both the size of the urban centers and the territories around them. It was therefore not feasible to concentrate all centers of production in one place (Henderson et al., 2017). To be sure, the first investments in early industrializers came in places with the most favorable natural geography – especially trading ports and fuel deposits, but also fertile land that would feed a populous city. Yet, upon reaching the natural limits of those cities, and with surplus available from the most productive places, early industrializers began to invest in secondary cities with somewhat less favorable geography (Hunt, 1986; Puga and Venables, 1996).[5] The success in the medium run by industrial elites interested in the development of integrated national markets leads to the surpassing (and eventual integration via inter-elite coalitions) of preexisting elites and the creation of a well-integrated network of urban centers, connected via railroads, that overcame the constraining effects of preexisting physical geographic differences. Such a strategy to overcome the limits on existing pools of local workers and consumers and to facilitate a broader distribution of manufactures brought, as a result, a relatively balanced geography of growth.

When increasing returns accrue to new industrial elites at the expense of the landed aristocracy, elites' heterogeneity increases and preferences diverge. Along with industrialization comes a competition between elites with clearly differentiated preferences over public goods and tax investments and structures (Lizzeri and Persico, 2004; Moore et al., 1993). The new industrial elites will successfully push for the expansion of markets both nationally and through international trade. Investments in transportation, in large part, reflect the political triumph of industrial elites in their quest for partial democracy at the expense of resisting, yet ultimately conceding to, traditional rural elites (Ansell and Samuels, 2014). Subsequently, as the economy becomes integrated and grows in complexity, capital elites have greater incentives than agricultural elites to invest in public goods such as health and education to improve worker

---

[5] In the case of England, the improvement of communications was under way well before industrialization consolidated. The Whig rule in the decades following the Glorious Revolution century undertook considerable investments in turnpikes and other improvements of travel and communication (Bogart, 2005; Pincus and Robinson, 2014). Industrialization reinforced and accelerated this process.

productivity (Beramendi et al., 2018; Hollenbach, 2019). The demand for human capital formation grows along with the demand for a better skilled and diversified labor force, as do the size and complexity of the bureaucracy associated with the growing role of the state as provider of order, communications, and services.

In early industrializers ($\lambda_C > \lambda_A \leq 1$), despite significant variation among them, industrial elites successfully accomplish the creation of national markets via large-scale infrastructure and public goods provision. This, in turn, translated into the early institutionalization of a sizable capacity stock. The growing costs of these investments triggers the expansion of two institutions critical to early industrialization efforts: credit systems and bureaucracies that underlie the capacity to sustain a stable flow of revenues.[6] Capitalists in early industrializers were harmed by tariffs and faced stiff resistance to increased land taxation (Mares and Queralt, 2015). Over time, the conflict between old and new elites becomes one about the political incorporation of labor into politics, a process driven by the sequential opening of the political arena by incumbent elites. The expansion of fiscal capacity was originally adopted under restricted suffrage, in part under the expectation that tax rates would not increase beyond those favored by capitalist elites (Aidt and Jensen, 2014; Beramendi and Queralt, 2014).[7] Eventually, industrial elites accept income taxation as the most lucrative and least distortionary of their unattractive revenue options.

2.4 The External Conquest of Space and Late Movers: Colonial Legacies, Spatial Concentration, and Capacity

Alongside the internal conquest of space, early industrialization also implied a change in the approach to external possessions by European metropoles. Large empires fueled the industrial revolution and spatial incorporation of the early industrializing nations. Proto-industrial empires (such as the British or the Dutch, and later, the Belgian, German, or French empires) coexisted with older ones, organized to a larger degree around mercantilist principles (Spain). Early industrializing empires, those who first prioritized λ_C over λ_A in the metropole, combined an internal conquest of space, triggering a balanced pattern of urbanization within their territories, and a sustained external conquest of

---

[6] In the English case, both pillars rested on another major institutional innovation emerging from the Glorious Revolution: annual budgets on which the executive had the monopoly to propose and Parliament had the monopoly to review and, if necessary, veto (Congleton, 2010; Cox, 2016).

[7] Though progressive direct taxation had important redistributive consequences over the twentieth century (Besley and Persson, 2013), pre-World War I income tax rates were relatively low (Aidt and Jensen, 2009; Seligman, 1914).

space, through colonies organized for the economic and geopolitical benefit of the metropole.

In concluding his 1917 essay on imperialism, Lenin (1999) assesses the link between the high stage of capitalism and imperialism in the following terms:

> Monopolies, oligarchy, the striving for domination and not for freedom, the exploitation of an increasing number of small or weak nations by a handful of the richest or most powerful nations – all these have given birth to those distinctive characteristics of imperialism which compel us to define it as parasitic or decaying capitalism. More and more prominently there emerges, as one of the tendencies of imperialism, the creation of the "rentier state," the usurer state, in which the bourgeoisie to an ever-increasing degree lives on the proceeds of capital exports and by "clipping coupons." It would be a mistake to believe that this tendency to decay precludes the rapid growth of capitalism. It does not. In the epoch of imperialism, certain branches of industry, certain strata of the bourgeoisie and certain countries betray, to a greater or lesser degree, now one and now another of these tendencies. On the whole, capitalism is growing far more rapidly than before; but this growth is not only becoming more and more uneven in general, its unevenness also manifests itself, in particular, in the decay of the countries which are richest in capital (Britain).

The exploitation of a large number of emerging nations by European powers had a long pedigree by 1917, about a century after most Spanish colonies in Latin America claimed their independence. Older mercantilist empires had shrunk in size well before the metropoles, or parts thereof, entered the industrial world.[8] By the time industrialization took place, their former colonies, now independent countries, entered the world arena under the growing influence of industrial empires, most notably Britain and increasingly the United States (Kohli, 2019).

England's transition from mercantilism to industrialism also took place amidst its imperial expansion. The two processes were tightly linked. England was ripe for industry at a time in which international trade underwent major structural changes. As Hobsbawm (1968, p. 30) puts it, "the traditional patterns of European expansion – Mediterranean, and based on Italian merchants and their associates, Spanish and Portuguese conquerors, or Baltic, based on German city-states – had perished in the great economic depression of the seventeenth century." Instead, growing markets in the North Sea and the North Atlantic expanded the demand for manufactures, themselves becoming cheaper

---

[8] By way of illustration, the first railroad line in the Iberian peninsula opened in 1848, between Barcelona and Mataro. By that time, the only remaining colonies of the Spanish Empire were a few Caribbean Islands, most prominently Cuba, the Philippines, and parts of Northern Africa.

and available in large quantities. At the same time, proto-industrial empires expanded their colonial presence, creating systems, such as slave-owned plantations, necessary for the production of such goods, and broadening the demand for manufactures. The expansion of trade and colonial rule through the 1700s led Hobsbawm to conclude that England's industrial economy "grew out of our commerce, and especially out of commerce with the underdeveloped world. And throughout the nineteenth century it was to retain this peculiar historical pattern: commerce and shipping maintained our balance of payments, and the exchange of overseas primary products for British manufactures was to be the foundation of our international economy" (Hobsbawm, 1968, p. 32). The internal conquest of space would not have been possible before the external one, and vice versa.

Across all cases, colonial rule consolidated very polarized economic and political geographies (Herbst, 2014). Broadly speaking, with the exception of a few states in the northern United States, colonies evolved under two regimes: mercantilist extraction or proto-industrial exchange of "goods for manufactures."

Lenin was correct in pointing to the interdependencies between the domestic needs of metropoles and the situation of the colonies. He was wrong in predicting that such interdependencies would lead to the "decay of the countries who are richest in capital." In relative terms, quite the opposite occurred, in large part because the legacy of spatial concentration associated with colonialism would hinder or prevent the effective development of state institutions in former colonies.

The external conquest by mercantilist empires led to an economic system that privileged both the cultivation of agricultural products and the extraction of natural resources, to be sent back to the Crown. Similarly, industrializing metropoles had the advantage to organize domestic and international markets to their advantage and to design colonial institutions according to their needs. Differences in modes of colonial rule notwithstanding, both types of empires shared a number of practices: the exploitation and displacement of indigenous populations associated with the production of primary goods and the extraction of natural resources (both facilitated by a favorable physical geography); the introduction in these territories of incipient forms of state administration and military control (Garfias et al., 2018); the design of infrastructure for the goals and needs of the metropole, often linked to a very small number of distribution centers; and the formation, around these centers, of a very concentrated economic and political elite (Huillery, 2009; Jedwab and Moradi, 2016; Roessler et al., 2020).

As a result, both imperial regimes left an important imprint on the patterns of spatial concentration of economic activities and political elites, ultimately shaping their calculus about public goods investments and capacity development. We turn now to analyze why, as opposed to early movers and their choice to prioritize λ_C over λ_A, key elites among late industrializers chose the opposite strategy, and with what consequences in terms of initial capacity stocks.

The legacy of colonial spatial concentration shapes elites' strategy in two ways. First, postcolonial elites had neither the will nor the ability to compete with the first movers of industrialization in the production of industrial goods. Late industrializers also started in a trailing position vis-á-vis early industrializers in production of finished goods. Rather, their comparative advantage was in the increasingly efficient production and distribution of commodities (Cai and Treisman, 2005; Cardoso and Faletto, 1979). The abundance of land and/or natural resources, coupled with a large pool of cheap labor, reduces the incentives for technological innovation in the areas of production (Allen et al., 2012; Baer, 1972; Edwards, 1993).

Second, postcolonial elites also lacked the capacity to overhaul the inherited allocation of space.[9] New public good investments are a way to exploit economic complementarities between the production and the distribution areas. The latter were determined by prior colonial investments in coastal areas for the purposes of military control and the distribution of commodities. The goal of agricultural elites in this historical context was to organize the new industrial sector such that it served their core interests (Kohli, 2004). Exercising their strong political leverage, they manage to mechanize agriculture in order to maintain their comparative advantage (Carlson, 2019; Haber, 2005). Industrial investments in export-oriented agricultural economies were meant to support, rather than upend, rural development. Given the benefits of mechanizing the agricultural economy, many agricultural elites added industrial portfolios in late industrializing nations (Collier and Collier, 2002; Hora, 2002). This strategy was further reinforced by the preferences of financial investors who were often of foreign origin and interested in exploiting the synergies between export oriented commodity producers and their own domestic markets (Kohli, 2019).

This process, in turn, points to a different link between industrialization and the spatial economics of agglomeration. Commodities are far more dependent on economic geography than on industrial production. Industrial production

---

[9] Preexisting infrastructure investments that provided the foundation for certain regions' prosperity also matter, as we discuss in the cases. Colonial governments' concentration of resources in capital cities in sub-Saharan Africa, for example, appear to matter tremendously to spatial investments (Boone and Simson, 2019).

may have started in places with favorable geography but could move out to places with less and less natural endowment. By contrast, commodity productivity depends on maximizing yield from favorable geography. Since public goods investments to build and link the new industrial cities depend on resources from the established urban centers, much of the nation was never incorporated in productive activity in late industrializers. Large sections of the new nations did not offer returns from favorable geography (Boone, 2012; Soifer, 2015). The potential benefits of building up competitor cities did not warrant the spatial redistribution (Mazucca, 2017). As a result, the internal conquest of space remains incomplete. The preexisting patterns of spatial polarization, a combination of physical constraints and colonial choices about location and space control, only become stronger (Cipolla, 2013; O'Rourke et al., 2010). In late industrializers, $\lambda_A > \lambda_C \leq 1$. Despite significant variation among them, rural elites successfully limit industrial investments to the needs of export-oriented agriculture and facilitate the concentration of associated financial and production activities in one major distribution point, thus increasing the polarizing effect of initial geographic endowments.

Railway improvements, for example, are made in a stark hub-and-spoke design, meant mainly to transport primary goods to distribution centers for export (Keeling, 1993).[10] Moreover, the industrialization of commodities requires lower investments in public goods than the production of human capital intensive manufactures. As a result, efforts to expand public education systems will also be lower (Lindert, 2004). Overall, the demand for investments in these cases is much narrower, concentrated in space, and smaller in size. Moreover, in many instances, late industrializers received both foreign direct investments in public infrastructure by core industrialized nations and had access to lines of credit that substituted for the need to invest in revenue-raising reforms.[11] Investments are led politically by export-oriented rural producers with an interest in controlled industrial development, the cost of which is funded largely from foreign sources. Jointly, these factors help explain why the provision of such public goods did not entail high levels of fiscal capacity in late industrializing nations. Importantly, these low initial investments

---

[10] For example, railway investments in Argentina, Brazil, and Mexico spurred economic growth in their respective agricultural sectors (Haber, 2005).

[11] The British, for example, made extensive investments in docks and ports, electrical power, and railways in Latin America (Stone, 1977). The availability of foreign direct investments to support targeted infrastructural developments suited elites well and had direct implications for the development of early capacity stocks. External funding reduces conflict over the cost allocation of investment decisions within an elite that features significant overlap across sectors. For a detailed empirical example of such an overlap in the cases of Argentina and Chile, see Paniagua (2018).

constrain subsequent efforts (Queralt, 2015), thereby shaping the dynamics of capacity divergence during the twentieth century.

2.5 The Dynamics of Capacity Divergence: Geography, Democracy, and War

Section 2.4 has analyzed how the combination of spatial concentration associated with colonialism and different waves of industrialization account for differences in capacity stocks across democracies. Central to this process are two factors that feed back into the divergence in capacity stocks over time: war and the bureaucracy-representation link.

A long tradition of research has highlighted the connection between interstate conflicts and state formation at various times in history. Tilly (1975) famously tied the balance of coercion and capital to the internal power balance and the specific form modern European states ended up with.[12] There is also compelling evidence that both World Wars facilitated the expansion of the state as provider of insurance, regulator of markets, and, critical to our argument, revenue collection. Scheve and Stasavage (2010, 2012), for example, show evidence that class conflict over progressive direct taxation did not typically emerge until World Wars I and II. More recently, Queralt (2019) also shows that the way wars are funded is critical to understanding the process of state formation: access to international credit crowds out the necessary institutional investments to consolidate capable fiscal bureaucracies even if states are involved in interstate conflict.

Interestingly, the nature of war makes the link between the internal and the external conquest of space most apparent and reinforces preexisting differences. World Wars I and II were, in part, a process of renewal of colonial empires, a rebalancing of the international economic and geopolitical dominance between competing European and, increasingly, North American powers (Hauner et al., 2017; Hobsbawm, 1989; Joll and Martel, 2013). From our perspective, these effects compound the legacy of war in terms of capacity stocks. Early industrializers are the great powers in conflict for either direct influence on colonies (WWI) or indirect control of large shares of the developing world (WWII).[13] This tension triggers very different dynamics in polities that,

---

[12] In a recent engagement with this line of work, Dincecco and Onorato (2018) point to urbanization as the linking mechanism between war and state formation in Europe.

[13] The only exception to this grouping is Russia/the Soviet Union, whose process of massive state-led industrialization took place primarily in the run-up to World War II (Gerschenkron, 1962; Kornai, 1992; Wheatcroft et al., 1986).

to begin with, depart from very different levels of capacity, with implications for the process of state consolidation and the nature of democracy.

Consider first the evolution of political conflict within early industrializing metropoles engaged in interstate conflict. By the time WWI arrives, the internal conquest of space is finalized and domestic politics has shifted from a conflict between rural landholder and liberal industrialist to a conflict between the latter and a complex web of organizations (socialist, communist, social-catholic) demanding higher levels of economic and political equality. The transition from a baron-led, faction-based, largely clientelistic power politics to a more institutionalized programmatic contest is well underway yet far from completed. The wars facilitated a rewrite of the social contract and changed the bargaining space among domestic actors. The universalization of franchise and the associated expansion of public goods created additional revenue demands. The acceptance by elites of the introduction and, more often, of an expanded implementation of both assets and progressive income taxation, helped meet these demands.

The unfolding of the *democratic class struggle* was jointly endogenous to the expansion of capacity that resulted from this process (Beramendi et al., 2018). After 1945, among early industrializers, the regular contention over who gets what became articulated around increasingly complex party organizations competing over the redistributive scope of regulation, public services, and the fiscal state. To be sure, remnants of prior forms of politics were alive and well in specific areas within these nations (more on this in Section 6), but among countries that industrialized early and took part in major interstate wars, the interaction between domestic and external conditions led, in relative terms, to the highest levels of capacity, progressivity, and redistribution.

The consolidation of the fiscal state among early industrializers, much like the preceding internal conquest of space, had strong implications for the rest of the world. The expansion of the welfare state among early industrializers coincided with a decline in their ability to hold direct control over former colonies and a significant redrawing of international influence with the onset of Cold War. As colonies became independent and the relative balance of power between empires changed, influence shifted from direct military control to indirect external economic and political influence. Yet one thing remained constant: external powers had little interest in the institutional modernization of colonies. The absence of an external push for state development in the former colonies of Latin America or Africa implied that the inherited domestic political and institutional dynamics remained (Centeno, 2002; Kohli, 2019, Queralt, 2019).

The combination of colonial legacies with smaller-scale wars and the rise of civil wars in late developers led to a different logic of political development, one that reinforces the constraining role of geography. Queralt (2019) shows that the external financing of interstate wars weakened bureaucracies and undermined state building in late developers. This divergence in capacity between early and late developers was apparent even prior to World War I, and it has persisted to the present. Post-World War II decolonization reinforced these trends in late industrializers, with transition to independence made under weak bureaucracies and a polarized economic and political geography that fed on each other.

The civil wars of the second half of the twentieth century further reinforced state-building dynamics in the late industrializers and former colonies. Civil wars accentuate preexisting social and geographical divisions, preventing the construction of social and political consensus that might overcome the limitations of geography. The efforts of states during civil wars are not focused on economic development. Resources that might otherwise fund national investments are instead devoted toward the internal conflict.

As argued in Section 2.1, the initial logic of late development is one in which economic geography informed investments in public goods, which were less needed with agricultural-linked industry, and the spatial distribution of public goods investments, which remained clustered in the places with the best land. The concentration of economic advantage and the rapid urban density in key distribution points gives way to a very different kind of politics.

To begin with, highly coordinated economic elites, with portfolio interests in both agricultural and the emerging industrial sectors, are wary of empowering the state. Largely tied to nonmobile assets, they fear independent bureaucracies capable of extracting more revenue in the future, and with some basis. Most elites in late industrializers were considering these investments in the middle years of the twentieth century. By this time, the expansion of the fiscal state in early industrializers would have been apparent to them. Therefore, they would not assume that fiscal capacity would remain the exclusive purview of elites – it would imply large-scale redistribution moving forward (Gottlieb, 2019; Hollenbach and Nascimiento de Silva, 2019; Suryanarayan, 2017). Their preference is much closer to a paper leviathan (Acemoglu and Robinson, 2019), a smaller state, with limited ability to enforce laws and regulations, with lower extractive capacity and a much weaker grasp over special interests and territories (Suryanarayan and White, 2021). Two important implications follow.

First, politics remains polarized spatially. Postcolonial elites, located in large cities, employ several instruments to ensure their survival in office. A steep gradient in favor of cities, particularly capital, in the provision and access to public goods (Bates, 2014; Pierskalla et al., 2017) benefits the elites in two ways: it reduces the likelihood of mobilization challenging the status quo and allows the capture, for their own benefit, of significant shares of the budget. At the same time, elites in highly populated areas secure the support of their counterparts in underpopulated areas outside the production-distribution trail by privileging their access to interregional transfers. Such access is often guaranteed through legislative malapportionment and helps reduce the formation of political coalitions in support of programmatic expansions of public goods and fiscal redistribution. As we analyze in Volume II, the latter is an important mechanism behind the persistence of the combination of polarized economic geographies and relatively weaker states.

Second, regarding the nature of democracy, politics remains, in relative terms, far less programmatic. Political competition features parties regularly engaged in "portfolio diversification," that is, a combination of broad programmatic proposals with the regular mobilization of voters via targeted club goods and clientelistic exchanges (Diaz-Cayeros et al., 2016; Magaloni et al., 2007). This is the case in both urban and rural areas, albeit with variations in the specific policy portfolios at work (Gans-Morse et al., 2014; Ichino and Nathan, 2013; Stokes et al., 2013).[14] This combination of mobilization strategies is both a reflection of lower levels of state capacity and a mechanism that ensures its perpetuation over time (Kasara and Suryanarayan, 2020). Mobilizing poor voters via targeted exchanges is cheaper and more effective than setting out to win support from them via a large-scale expansion of public goods with uncertain future returns (Amat and Beramendi, 2020). At the same time, the pervasiveness of such a strategy renders state institutions much more prone to capture. Elites retain control over territorial strongholds via partial, targeted exchanges with voters, which in turn secures their ability to capture regulations and block attempts to expand the scope of public services and insurance systems. As a result, the fiscal state is weaker in scope and more regressive in nature. The dominant fiscal architecture in these cases transitions from tariffs to indirect taxes, with a relatively weaker role for direct income taxes relative to the fiscal structures in early industrializers (Wibbels et al., 2003).

2.6 The Importance of Mixed Cases

Our analysis of the dynamics of capacity divergence so far has emphasized two factors: the spatial legacies derived from colonialism and different types

---

[14] Clientelistic exchanges might remain part of the parties' portfolios due to social choice problems related to the tensions between rural and urban interests within the same parties (Kitschelt, 2000).

of industrialization, and the role of international conflict as a booster of the initial divergence in capacity stocks. In ideal terms, political conflict in war-waging industrializing metropoles saw the early rise of an industrial elite and a democratic conflict over economy and political equality centered around the provision of public goods. By contrast, elites in former colonies with lesser exposure to military conflict managed to preserve their relative advantage by limiting the scope of industrialization and institutionalizing very high levels of social and spatial polarization.

To capture the different mechanisms at work in our analysis, it is worth exploring what happens when: (1) large levels of spatial polarization coexist with early industrialization and; (2) geopolitical motives gain salience in a context of late industrialization.

Case (1): Polarized Geography among Early Industrializers

The cases in (1) are captured by the top-right cell (labeled "Mixed") in Figure 2, a scenario where both $\lambda_A > 1$ and $\lambda_C > 1$ coexist in different areas within the same polity. These are cases in which the scale of the nation allows for different types of industrialization to coexist and/or early industrializers are geographically concentrated and unable to seize political control of the central state institutions.

For areas with conditions that enabled early industrialization, such as the US Northeast or Spain's Catalonia, the incentives are similar to early industrializers. Industrial elites see value in public goods investments to improve worker productivity and deliver products to export markets. The tension comes because of centralized investments in fiscal capacity and public goods that would disproportionately benefit the industrialized areas. The costs of those investments would fall heavily on the industrialized regions, but the expanded centralized fiscal capacity might also be used for investments not preferred by industrial elites down the road. Thus, both groups are hesitant about centralized fiscal capacity – agricultural elites may not value the public goods investments sought by industrial elites, and industrial elites worry that the resources extracted from their regions could be reallocated to the agricultural regions. Ultimately, the influence of the agricultural regions and economic disparities between the agricultural and industrial areas remains a source of tension in all central government negotiations.

Agricultural elites may feel particularly threatened in mixed cases where competitive industrial and competitive, export-oriented agricultural regions coexist. Agricultural elites in the latter also conflict with uncompetitive domestic agriculture, which favors protectionism alongside industrializing elites in late developers. The eventual "victory" of industrial elites in political and economic competition is prolonged and often incomplete. These nations will have long-term regional conflict even while having economies partially resemble early industrializers.

Such conflict also conditions the nature of logrolls. In cases with a sizable stock of territory controlled by elites benefiting from low-wage rural labor, these elites will try to protect their relative position at all costs, whereas the new elites will push for the territorial expansion of markets. Old rural elites will only endorse increases in fiscal capacity from which they are able to reap large benefits (such as military expenditures), and will resist any expansion of the central government that threatens their status quo (e.g., Alston and Ferrie [1999] on the US South). If pressured, they will accept the expansion of the federal government into new territories in exchange for the preservation of their own autonomy to control production and politics in their areas. New elites will successfully push for fiscal expansion to support the necessary investments for the creation of a sufficiently large market. The specific evolution of the fiscal history of the country will depend on the political conflict between industrial and rural elites that are *de facto* entrenched in different parts of of the territory and on which specific elite seizes control of the central government and for how long. In these cases we would expect intermediate levels of capacity to coexist with high levels of geographic economic disparity.

Case (2): Geopolitical Tensions in a Context of Late Industrialization

Of course, a subset of late industrializers has emerged in which the industrial elite won out, and patterns of spatial growth have become less concentrated over time. In line with a well-established stream of research that sees war and international conflict as a major source of fiscal development and institutional modernization, one path to overcome the industrialization gap stems out of pressures emerging directly out of geopolitical needs. It is a process that typically unfolds under autocratic conditions, one in which the resistance by landed elites toward economic and political modernization is overcome by military leaders' concerns about geopolitical threats. Interestingly, this process is prevalent in cases such as South Korea and Taiwan, or earlier in history, Japan, in which physical geography conditions are not suitable for the development of large-scale agriculture.

South Korea represents a case of late development that contrasts with our account of agricultural dominance, regional cleavages, high inequality, and biased voting systems that privilege rural elites. South Korea's industrialization process was shaped by military. In the aftermath of the Korean War, South Korea's economic development intensified in the mid-twentieth century with a military dictatorship supported by the American military that nullified the (already comparatively weak) antidevelopment agricultural elite through land redistribution (Albertus, 2015). After land reform South Korea's agriculture was neglected, and inequality declined dramatically (Pan et al., 1980). The explicit military aim was to eliminate this political coalition against industrialization and to simultaneously reduce economic inequality that stood as a barrier to human capital investment (Haggard, 1990). The military government invested in the creation of national education systems and infrastructure that brought broad opportunity via education and full employment.

South Korea underwent a relatively smooth and early transition toward export-oriented industrialization that brought dramatic growth to the country (Haggard, 1990). The country grew at an unprecedented pace in the years that followed this transition to export competition (Haggard, 1990). The effects of openness on regional convergence are widely acknowledged (Henderson, 2002). While countries such as Argentina, Brazil, and Mexico maintained high barriers to trade long after their efforts at state-led industrialization began, South Korea quickly moved toward openness and international competition (Haggard, 2018). Most attribute South Korea's willingness to shift quickly toward export competition to decision-making by the industrialization-oriented military government, the coercive control of labor, and the elimination of resistance from the unproductive agricultural sector (Shin, 1998). Kuznets (1988, p. S11) also views these decisions as supported by the global economic climate: "Korea's phenomenal export expansion from the mid-1960s to the late 1970s occurred before the worldwide recession and rising protectionism dimmed prospects of replication by latecomers who might want to adopt the Korean model."

The government-led push for industrialization, largely driven as well by military concerns, was the dominant feature in both the Soviet Union and China as well. Contrary to Korea or Japan, both Russia and China had plenty of land suitable for large-scale agricultural production, land that was woefully under-exploited by traditional landed elites in both cases (Moon, 2014; Tang, 1979). The combination of military conflicts, and its burden on extremely poor populations, extreme inequalities, and the mobilization by communist parties led to revolutionary takeovers in both cases. The net result of these revolutions was the effective removal, often in actual existential terms, of the land aristocracy, thus paving the way for a process of state-led development. This process, again, was largely driven by military priorities, involved much higher levels of industrial and technological investment than was the case among proto-democratic late industrializers, and contributed to reshape, in a top-down process, the economic geography of both countries (Evans, 2012).

2.7 Spatial Inequality and Capacity: Summary of Hypotheses

Our argument in this book focuses on the origins of spatial inequalities and the implications of the latter for capacity development. We now link our argument to specific hypotheses guiding our empirical analysis. The logic of early political and economic development is one that works against preexisting geographical economic differences. The internal conquest of space, the extensive penetration of territories of early investments in infrastructure, and the consolidation of integrated national labor and consumption markets lead to a relatively more balanced process of agglomeration around a large number of urban centers. At the same time, the scope of redistribution helps bridge the gap between rich and poorer citizens with relatively similar effectiveness across the entire polity. Redistribution operates similarly within and across subnational units. Thus, while major structural transformations clearly have an asymmetric impact in different parts of the polity, highly capable states are able to partially contain their polarizing impact and by and large reduce the scope of interregional inequalities (Carrascal-Incera et al., 2020).

By contrast, the logic of late political and economic development is one that derives from and reinforces preexisting patterns of spatial inequalities. As elaborated earlier, the institutional legacies of the external conquest of space by early movers and the constraints on the type of industrialization within late movers facilitated a process built primarily around a small number of urban centers and regions, with heavy concentration of production in the "primate" city (Henderson, 2002; Puga, 1998). The elites in these regions had disproportionate influence in national policy, often through logrolls with the elites of less advanced areas, and limited the scope of fiscal extraction, the (related) progressivity of the fiscal system, and the expansion of public services (Ardanaz and Scartascini, 2013). As a result, interpersonal and interregional inequalities trace each other closely. Faced with structural transformations, weak fiscal states only work to exacerbate and reinforce preexisting regional inequalities.

Figure 4 captures the first empirical implications emerging from our argument (formally stated in hypothesis 1 and hypothesis 2 in what follows). It shows that the timing of industrialization is a key indicator of whether regional inequality is high or low in a nation, and whether natural economic endowments are strong indicators of regional productivity in the long term. Early industrialization lowered regional inequalities through territorial penetration and investments outside the regions with the best physical geography. Late

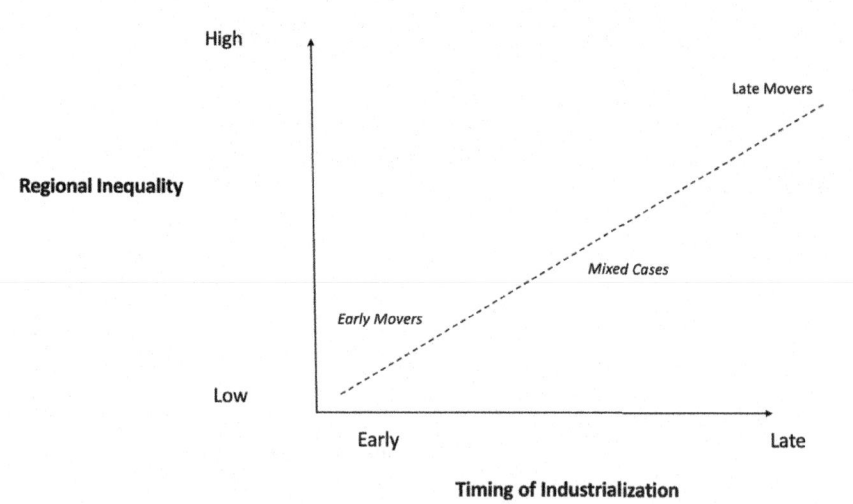

Figure 4 Implications for regional inequality.

industrialization reinforced natural physical endowments, leading in most cases to increased regional economic polarization. Over time, these regional inequalities create distributive tensions that limit central tax collection (Beramendi, 2012), central government spending (Lee and Rogers, 2019a), and, as we show in Volume II, central government efforts to equilibrate regions and reduce regional inequalities in the long run.

H1: The later in time the industrial development, the higher the levels of interregional economic inequality.

An additional implication of our logic concerns the relationship between natural endowments and interregional inequalities. Recall from Figure 5 that geography is not destiny. At the same time, skewed natural geography both underpins late industrialization and sees its polarizing effects reinforced by it by virtue of the combination between the internal and the external conquest of space. Accordingly:

H2: Natural economic endowments are a stronger predictor of levels of interregional inequalities in late industrializers as opposed to early industrializers.

Our argument also points to a direct connection between spatial economic skew and capacity development. The combination of internal and the external conquest of space by early movers shaped capacity investments in both early and late industrializers. In the former, metropoles engaged in interstate wars and, where the democratic class struggle consolidated early, capacity stocks developed early. In the latter, former colonies with skewed economic geography and incomplete development of programmatic politics, capacity stocks

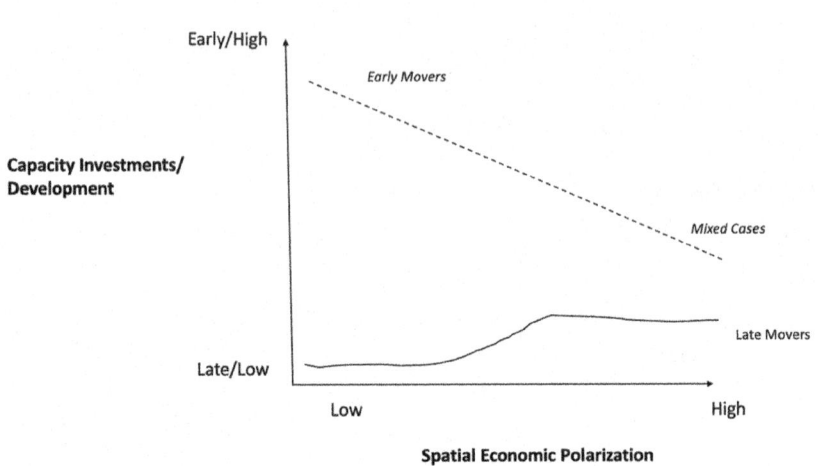

Figure 5 The origins of capacity differentials.

grew weak and territorially constrained. Figure 5 takes stock of our analysis of the origins of differential state capacity and displays graphically our third hypothesis.

H3: The higher the geographic polarization and the later in time the industrial development, the smaller the investments in capacity.

3 Empirical Strategy

We approach our empirical analysis according to the hypotheses presented in Section 2.7. We begin with the analysis of hypotheses 1 and 2 on the spatial implications of different waves of industrialization (Sections 4 and 5).

First, we use available historical evidence on the evolution of subnational economies during the period of industrialization in our cases and other nations with available data. We draw upon historical data on the distribution of regional productivity to show how regions diverged in economic terms during the industrialization process.[15] We also show evidence of government efforts to encourage regional economic convergence by investing in integrated transportation networks that brought raw materials and workers to production sites, products to ports and markets, and linked products to consumers across the nation. We contrast these efforts with many late industrializing cases in which industrialization was concentrated in a central city and government efforts to develop infrastructure and markets reinforced the primacy of that central

---

[15] Appendix 1 provides a detailed list of the original data set we collected to enable our empirical strategy.

city. We piece together historical evidence to present a stylized account of early industrialization as a process that encouraged more balanced economic geography. Late industrialization, in comparison, reinforces uneven economic geography and results in more skewed subnational economic outcomes than those provided by nature alone.

Second, to link this historical overview with a more systematic assessment of the hypotheses, our efforts draw upon a new, global data set of subnational economic geography and economic outcomes. This is the first effort to document these patterns in a sample of countries that spans level of development, global region, economic structure, and historical experience. We provide approachable data visualization and empirical results consistent with broad historical trends.

Across the board, we show a pattern of evidence through multiple indicators, multiple specifications, and multiple levels of analysis. We take care to consider endogenous processes by using exogenous measures of economic geography as our primary explanatory variables. The result is intended not as the definitive causal word on the large-scale processes that we examine but rather as a consistent story to weave together complex dynamics.

Our regression models are cross-sectional because our indicators of subnational variation in economic endowments are static. We regress these economic endowment measures on our spatial inequality and capacity-dependent variables, holding constant a parsimonious set of controls. Our sample sizes are necessarily small, given we are using a cross section of nations. However, our models have the virtue of featuring plausibly exogenous independent variables (natural geography indicators) in relation to our dependent variables. Moreover, given the long-run processes we describe, we expect a relatively stable cross section – that levels of spatial inequality and capacity persist over time.

Sections 6 and 7 turn to hypothesis 3. In Section 6 we provide a first illustration of the links between spatial inequality and the politics of capacity development. We focus on the economic composition of elites in a mixed case, the United States, and show how states with different industrialization paths yield distinct socioeconomic composition in the legislatures that subsequently anchor states' fiscal structures.

Section 7 then turns to assess the relationship between geographic economic inequalities and capacity development. As in Sections 4 and 5, we first provide a historical overview of a few key representative experiences and then provide a more systematic quantitative assessment of hypothesis 3.

Before we present our empirical findings, we provide additional details on our measurement strategy, our approach to potential alternative channels, and our selection of robustness tests.

3.1 Measuring Economic Endowments

Our main variables focus on variation in subnational physical geography. To capture "exogenous" natural economic geography, we collected measures of agricultural endowments and trade access at fine-grained levels of geography using Geographic Information Systems (GIS) (Henderson et al., 2017). We aggregate these economic geography measures to two administrative levels (the first and second) and "exogenous" grid cells. We then calculate subnational variation in these values (Rogers, 2016).

One of the most obvious physical features related to economic development is soil conditions conducive to agriculture (Sachs, 2003). We employ *Grow Days*, the length, in days, of the growing period from FAO (2012), and a *Land Suitability* for agriculture indicator, measured as the predicted value of the likelihood that a given parcel of land would be under cultivation using four measures of climate and soil, from Ramankutty et al. (2002). In addition to these agriculture-specific measures, we capture *Precipitation* as the long-run (1960–90) average of rainfall available from Willmott and Matsuura (2012); *Elevation* in meters, from Isciences (2008); and Temperature, the long-run (1960–90) average available from UEA-CRU et al. (2013) based on Mitchell and Jones (2005).

We also include variables focused on access to natural trade routes, particularly via water routes that may account for economic differences. *Coastal Access*, *Lake Access*, *River Access*, and *Harbor Access* measure the average distance from the cells within the region to the nearest coast, large lake, navigable river, and natural harbor (Henderson et al., 2017).

For our main economic endowments measures, we follow Galor et al. (2009) to conduct a principal components analysis (PCA) to construct component variables usable in our regressions.[16] Our economic suitability variables are in many cases highly correlated, which may impact the estimates in our analysis and provide "redundant" information to capture economic endowments. We also show similar results with subcomponents of our PCA indicators in Appendix 7.

We utilize the first-level administrative region (GEOLEV1) as our subnational unit of focus for our sample. This variable refers to states in cases such as the USA, Mexico, and Brazil, to provinces in places such as Canada and Argentina, to departments in Colombia, to regions in Russia, and the Nomenclature of Territorial Units for Statistics (NUTS2) level 2 designation in European Union

---

[16] See summary statistics and components loadings from our PCA and alternative PCA calculations in the Appendix.

countries. The first-level administrative region is typically the most important administrative and political unit.

3.2 Measuring Spatial Inequalities

We also employ subnational GDP and population data for every country in the world with available data. This time series database includes nearly 100 countries, most with observations from 1980 to 2011. The most difficult task was collecting these data for non-European countries. This required searching the national accounts data of every country in the world in detail to find, if available, gross domestic project divided by state, province, region, or department, depending on the nation. These data are not straightforward to locate on any national accounts website but rather often involve extensive searches of datasets and publications by national statistical agencies. Moreover, to obtain region-level population, we had to look through the census and population projections of each nation.[17]

Our theoretical interest is in the distribution of endowments and productivity across geographic space. We focus on two concepts in our measures of subnational dispersion – the coefficient of variation (*COV*) and the region-adjusted Gini coefficient (*ADGINI*). Dispersion measures capture the extent of spread of values (e.g., natural economic endowments or economic productivity) across regions.

COV and ADGINI are dispersion measures with different properties (Lee and Rogers, 2019b; Lessmann, 2012). These indicators are explained in what follows, using economic productivity (regional GDP per capita) as an example. The most simple, easy-to-interpret, regional variation measure is COV. COV is a dispersion measure without analytical weights and is constructed as shown in Eq. (1):

$$\text{COV} = \frac{1}{\bar{y}} \left(\frac{1}{n} \sum\nolimits_{i=1}^{n} (\bar{y} - y_i)^2 \right)^{1/2}, \tag{1}$$

where $\bar{y}$ denotes the country's average GDP per capita, y_i is per capita GDP of region i, and n is the number of subnational units. COV is a widely used measure in the literature on regional economic growth and convergence (Barro and Sala-i Martin, 1992; Sala-i Martin, 1996).

Similar to COV, the region-adjusted Gini coefficient (ADGINI) captures the dispersion of productivity across subnational regions. Unlike COV, ADGINI

---

[17] The countries with available subnational GDP per capita data, the name and number of the first-level administrative units, the time coverage, and the sources of the variables are detailed in our online Appendix.

retains meaningful information about the type of distribution. In ADGINI, additional weight is given to a region's per capita productivity as it veers father away from the mean of the interregional productivity distribution. This weighted value makes the inequality measure more sensitive to changes in the upper or lower tail of this distribution. ADGINI is calculated as shown in Eq. (2):

$$\text{ADGINI} = \frac{2\sum_{i=1}^{n} iy_i}{n\sum_{i=1}^{n} y_i} - \frac{n}{n-1}, \tag{2}$$

where y_i is the GDP per capita for region i, and n is the number of subnational units.

We calculate spatial dispersion measures for our natural economic geography indicators and for our measures of subnational economic productivity. We focus on COV for the natural geography measures and use both COV and ADGINI to measure spatial dispersion in economic productivity.

3.3 Measuring Capacity

To measure capacity we use a range of common indicators for tax collection and state capacity. First, we use the tax-to-GDP ratio and the direct tax share of total taxes from the Government Revenue Dataset (GRD) created by the International Center for Tax and Development (Prichard, 2016). For total tax revenue, we employ both their general government revenue (% GDP) and central government revenue (% GDP) measures. Direct taxes on income are the most difficult taxes to collect from a capacity perspective, which makes them a valuable indicator of state administrative capability and effort (Rogers and Weller, 2014). Direct taxation is also associated with high levels of overall taxation and efforts to address inequality via state redistribution. These tax measures are compiled from all available international sources, including the IMF Government Finance Statistics (GFS), IMF International Finance Statistics (IFS), the OECD, the UN's Economic Commission on Latin America, the UN's African Economic Outlook, and IMF country reports.

We show results using the state capacity measuring legibility adapted by Lee and Zhang (2017) from research in demography. D'Arcy and Nistotskaya (2017) and Lee and Zhang (2017) argue that census data provide a reasonable measure of the state's knowledge of its citizens, what they call "legibility," a crucial indicator of state capacity. They measure state information using the Myers' Score, an indicator of smoothness in population data. When population data is not smooth, this indicates weak legibility of the state because they have not provided that citizen with a record of birth or identification that indicates age, or enumerators cannot safely survey citizens. We do not use the legibility variable as our primary measure of capacity because it is only available in country census years.

3.4 Alternative Channels

In our regression estimates, we include standard controls that predict investments in public goods and tax capacity (Ardanaz and Scartascini, 2013; Timmons, 2005). Given that we opt for cross-sectional models in most cases, we employ for a parsimonious and limited set of controls: GDP per capita, partisanship of the chief executive, and experience with major international war.

Economic development entails a growth in the size of the economy, the size of government, and the level of taxable activity. We include the logged value of GDP per capita (adjusted for purchasing power parity) from the Penn World Tables to control for economic development.

Partisanship of the government may also influence investments in public goods and tax capacity. Leftist parties with working class constituents will be more likely to want a redistributive government, both in terms of provision of public goods and expansion of the welfare state (cf. Korpi [2006]). To redistribute high levels of income, the state needs high levels of available revenue. For most countries, this requires extracting high levels of taxation. According to this logic, when leftist governments are in power, they should increase tax capacity. To capture this effect, we employ a dummy variable for when the head of government is leftist from Brambor et al. (2013). We recognize that this measure is a very rough indicator of the true political power of the left in many nations, but this variable is the only one available with wide coverage of developed and developing nations for our sample period.

An important strand of research has argued that war is a major driver of the development of state capacity, including tax capacity (Dincecco, 2011; Scheve and Stasavage, 2010; Tilly, 1992). According to these arguments, when countries engage in mass mobilization for war, they are forced to reorganize and to change their relationship to society to extract more revenue. This entails a considerable improvement in the administrative power of the state (Mann, 1984; Tilly, 1992). It may also require the broadening of the base and progressivity of taxation to appeal to lower-income conscripts to the war (Scheve and Stasavage, 2010; Stasavage, 2005). We include a variable that captures the legacy of war on tax capacity. This is a dummy variable measuring 1 if that nation passed what Scheve and Stasavage consider a major mobilization of 2 percent of the population serving in the military during a time of war.

3.5 Robustness

In every analysis, we show robustness in our results with multiple dependent variables for (1) subnational inequality (coefficient of variation in subnational GDP per capita, Gini coefficient in subnational GDP per capita) and (2) fiscal capacity (total tax revenue % of GDP, central tax revenue % of GDP, direct tax revenue (% total tax revenue), Myers' Score of census "legibility"). The idea is to show a consistent pattern in the results that is not dependent on a particular operationalization of the concept.

In the Appendix, we make additional efforts to demonstrate the robustness of the trends we document. In addition to using multiple dependent variables in each analysis, we try different approaches to the independent variables. We conduct our analysis at three different geographic levels to demonstrate the results are not driven by the unit selection (Lee and Rogers, 2019b). We show results for the second administrative level in Appendix 3. Finally, we test our results using grid cell data to see whether our results hold under "random" subunit borders. Specifically, we use the grid cell values from Henderson et al. (2017, p. 371). Their data are converted "to a grid of 1/4-degree cells, with each cell covering approximately 770 square kilometers (297 square miles) at the Equator, decreasing with the cosine of latitude." They argue the 1/4-degree scale structure economizes the processing power required to work with spatial data. It reduces concerns with spatial autocorrelation that we might have at higher at finer grid cell scales.

We also include analyses with samples that only include countries with substantial industrialization at the end of our data set (2010). In those analyses, we exclude countries with less than 30 percent industrial employment in 2010 in Appendix 4. To be sure our analysis is not contingent on our operationalization of the early or late timing of industrialization at 1950, we move the window on the timing of industrialization back to 1945 and up to 1955 in Appendix 5.

As discussed in Section 3.1, we construct the economic endowments indicators in several ways in Appendix 6. We include models with the first component and additional models with both the first and second components in our principal components analysis. We also include our direct measures of agricultural suitability and trade access (not their PCA values) in our models and receive consistent results.

Our main models feature cross-sectional means of time series values. We also run our models with yearly data, with year fixed effects in Appendix 7. In Appendices 8–10 we add additional controls for democracy, globalization, federalism, levels of physical geographic endowments, and natural resource revenue. Our results are consistent across these specifications. Finally, given that many of our results depend on interaction terms, we also test for linear assumption and common support in Appendix 11.

4 How Geography and Industrialization Shape Spatial Inequalities

The top 443 cities in the world, by population density, are in the developing world (Demographia, 2019). Cities 444 (Athens, Greece) and 452 (Bilbao, Spain) lay within late industrializers by our definition. The first city in an early industrializing nation is London at spot 482, with Vienna not far behind at 505. Depending on how you count the size of cities by population, either 6 or 19 of the top 100 in the world are in what most would consider advanced industrial democracies (Demographia, 2019). The more generous definition includes US metropolitian areas rather than city boundaries.

Why would urbanization, the hallmark of industrialization and development, be so clustered in space in late industrializing nations? Why would cities in late developers grow so large and dense in comparison to those in early industrializing nations? These questions point to the different nature of spatial organization in early versus late industrializing nations. Changes in technology, mostly in transportation, storage containerization, and refrigeration made possible much larger cities (Henderson et al., 2017). These innovations came from the early industrializers and enabled a different pattern of spatial development in the countries that industrialized in their wake. We argue that the clustering in space of late industrializers, and the emergent regional inequality associated with these patterns, prove to be an enormous political problem for investments in the central government. Once a particular city and region have developed far beyond the levels of its nation's periphery, the nation's subunits have a difficult time coordinating at the national level for common projects. Most importantly, they have difficulty agreeing to investments in central fiscal capacity that underlie common investments and long-term efforts to equalize opportunity and outcomes across people and space.

According to this logic, both the underlying, exogenous economic geography and the timing of industrialization are crucial to understanding whether the conflict over centralized state capacity proves enduring. The underlying geography shapes the costs and benefits to the nation of investment in public goods throughout the national territory. If the quality of the nation's geography is relatively equally spread, there is not a natural centralization problem. However, a man-made centralization problem may occur if early investments in infrastructure, such as by a colonial power, set a particular region far above the others (Roessler et al., 2020). Countries with relatively even economic geography through the territory should have a better chance at overcoming political resistance to state capacity, all else equal. The timing of industrialization is critical to understanding whether the centralization challenge brought on by uneven geography can be overcome. In early industrializers, (lack of) technology favored more spatially distributed development, lowering the conflict over centralization for state capacity. Late industrializers, on the other hand, saw the effect of economic geography reinforced by the growth of megacities in the most valuable land in the territory, with the rise of technology allowing that city to grow beyond what is seen in early industrializers.

In this section we describe, using historical analysis, case studies, and cross-national data, how geography and the timing of industrialization shape the spatial patterns of development and productivity around the world. We begin with a sketch of different conditions – early industrializers with relatively even economic endowments across space in comparison with early developers with uneven geography, and late industrializers with even versus uneven geography– for their different patterns of spatial development and long-run spatial inequalities. We integrate vignettes for how the spatial pattern of development proceeded in our four country cases – the UK, USA, Argentina, and South Korea. Throughout this section, we provide evidence, consistent with hypothesis 1, that late industrialization is linked to higher spatial inequalities.

4.1 Early Industrializers

When the demand for technological innovation emerges outside of the control of the landed aristocracy, elites are heterogeneous in their assets and preferences. Industrialization is driven by a competition between elites with clearly differentiated preferences over public goods and tax investments and tax structures (Beramendi et al., 2018; Lizzeri and Persico, 2004). Sectoral and portfolio ownership are differentiated early in the process, with new industrial elites supporting higher levels of infrastructural investment and public goods provision. Assuming a stock of scientific knowledge, a favorable legal environment, and the existence of natural transport networks that secure a minimum size of the initial market, increasing returns will lead to rapid rise of manufacturing, as occurred in North England or the American Iron Belt (Engerman and Sokoloff, 1997; Krugman, 1991). This leads to a process of political and economic competition between old and new elites, the result of which depends on the initial stock of areas highly dependent on low-cost agricultural labor. The stock of low-wage labor matters for the relative balance of power between the old and the new industrial elites.

The success in the medium run by industrial elites interested in the development of integrated national markets leads to the surpassing (and eventual integration via inter-elite coalitions) of preexisting elites and the creation of a well-integrated network of urban centers, connected via railroads, that overcame the constraining effects of preexisting physical geographic differences. When the scale of the nation allows for different types of industrialization to coexist (USA, Australia) and/or early industrializers are geographically concentrated and unable to seize political control of the central state institutions (Spain), the process unfolds more slowly.

In contrast, when the stock of low-wage labor is relatively small, the new industrial elites will successfully push for the expansion of markets both nationally and through international trade. This success will bring about the fast expansion of public goods and infrastructural investments along, which reflect in large part the political triumph of industrial elites in their quest for partial democracy at the expense of resisting traditional rural elites (Ansell and Samuels, 2014). In these cases, industrialization spreads through a larger share of the territory along with the expansion of transportation networks that both create a national market and serve the early development of manufacturing exports.

Other things being equal, the level of fiscal extraction necessary to support these investments becomes relatively higher as a share of the economy as a result. The cumulative effect of territorial scope of the industrialization process and the full incorporation of workers (and women) into politics after World War I explain in large part why the levels of fiscal capacity are at their highest in cases such as the UK.

SPATIAL ECONOMIC INTEGRATION: RAIL DEVELOPMENT IN THE UK

Efforts to maximize the benefits of industrialization required investments in public goods to integrate national markets. Integrating national markets was crucial to allow for the easy transport of inputs into the industrial process (labor, raw materials, energy, machinery) to colocate. Once these factors were brought together, these finished products needed to be distributed to the internal and, especially external, markets. The primary technology used to move goods and people in the industrialization process was railroad transportation. As Rostow (1959, pp. 302–303) argues: "The introduction of the railroad has been historically the most powerful single initiator of take-offs. It was decisive in the United States, Germany and Russia. ... Perhaps most important for the take-off itself, the development of railways has led on to the development of modern coal, iron, and engineering industries."

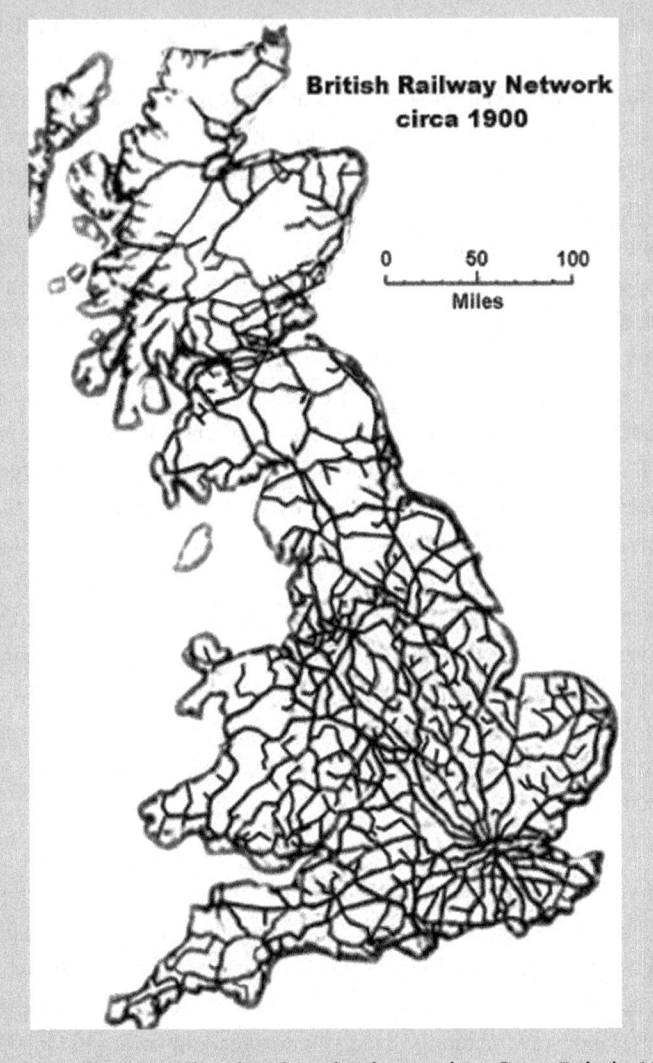

Figure 6 Railroads and national market integration: Great Britain 1900.

Countries faced decisions over how to invest in the railroad networks, which reflected the intensity of their efforts at national integration. In early industrializers we saw massive investments in railroads to encompass the nation and to incorporate geographic areas in a fully connected, integrated, and flexible rail network. Britain serves as an example of rail integration for a national market. Figure 6 shows the nation's rail network in 1881.

Clearly, nearly the full extent of Britain was incorporated into the rail network, with minor stations connected to each other and to the larger urban hubs. This integration allowed for movement of people and goods across the nation and allowed the later industrializing parts of the nation to catch up to the rest.

Dispersion of economic endowments clearly mattered to the spatial investments even in early industrializers. In countries such as the United States, initial industrialization was limited to the parts of the nation with favorable trade access, access to energy, and nascent capital markets but relatively poor agricultural land, namely the Northeast. The parts of the nation with good agricultural land, namely the Southeast, saw the continued domination of agricultural elites. Industrialization did not quickly spread to these areas, and they maintained lower investments in public goods that persist to this day. Importantly, the size and economic diversity of a country like the United States enabled uneven development and also brought significant regional conflict (Bensel et al., 2000). Regional conflict permeated debates over centralized investment in fiscal capacity, as we discuss in Section 7 with the US federal income tax. Yet these debates were clearly overcome in the United States more than in countries with similar endowments, such as Argentina or Brazil. We attribute those differences to the bounty of early industrialization that provided surplus enough to partially overcome political resistance to central capacity, without which the industrialized parts of that nation could not maximize growth.

SPATIAL ECONOMIC BIFURCATION: RAIL DEVELOPMENT IN THE USA
The United States is a clear case of uneven industrialization – the Northeast and Midwest were early industrializers and the Southeast only industrialized in the mid-twentieth century. These regions have coexisted with considerable difficulty, including entering into civil war over the South's agriculture-based economic structure built upon slavery. The USA is thus a mixed case for our theory – one in which early industrialization was present, but its spread was incomplete. The tension around centralization, always focal in the American context, reflected these divergent economic paths and conflicting elite interests.

Figure 7 Railroads and national market integration: USA 1900.

Uneven industrialization in the US context was apparent in the spread of railroad infrastructure. In Figure 7, we see evidence of the concentration of investments in the Northern states, and the relative lack of integration of the South into the national economy. To be sure, the South was connected for the purposes of commodity extraction. However, we do not see the dense networks of rail in the South that were intended to bring workers to labor markets and to ship goods to consumers. Like the map of Argentina's railroads in Figure 8, we see a pattern of linkages bringing commodities to the North for final production. The US South, like the Global South, did not provide finished goods but commodity inputs. The eventual decision to integrate the South into national markets was one fully undertaken in the boom times of the post-World War II era (Jaworski, 2017).

To summarize, in early industrializers, despite significant variation among them:

1. Industrial elites successfully accomplish the creation of national markets via large-scale infrastructure and public goods provision, thus reducing the polarizing effect of initial geographic endowments.
2. This process is incomplete in early industrializers with uneven economic geography, resulting in enduring tension across regions that is mollified by relatively high levels of development.

To fund these large-scale investments and manage politically the incorporation of larger pools of voters, early industrializing nations invested in the
development of fiscally capable, and in the long run relatively more progressive, states. This fiscal capacity also enabled the politics of redistribution, the
subject of Volume II. The presence of these capable state organizations and
fiscal bureaucracies allows for the reallocation of income though the political
process and facilitates the relative reduction of both interpersonal and spatial
inequalities.

4.2 Late Industrializers with High Dispersion

When the structure of agricultural labor costs delays the demand for technological innovation, traditional rural elites remain largely unchallenged and control
the process of industrialization. As a result we see relatively higher levels of
elite homogeneity, that is, the same set of elites own assets across sectors and/or
industries,[18] and, importantly, much lower levels of competition and far greater
levels of geographic concentration and economic polarization. To the extent
that a national market emerges, it is highly asymmetric and tilted toward the
interests of dominant locations, often the "primate" city. In a nutshell, late
industrialization reinforces the polarizing effects of geography. The process
works as follows.

Low-labor-cost agriculture exhibits high levels of economic concentration,
largely driven by initial geographic endowments. Economic production within
the country tends to be dominated by a few economic poles within the same
sector of production, leading to continued dominance of primary sector elites.
Under these circumstances, rural elites are free to impose their first preferences
for status quo levels of public goods investments. Demand for technological
modernization is low (as there is an oversupply of cheap labor), and elites have
the capacity to protect a very skewed distribution of immobile assets. As a
result, demand for public goods will be historically low, limited to their specific distribution needs (and so will be the revenue collection efforts to fund
them). When investments occur, they carry a legacy of weak state institutions

---

[18] Of course, there is a fair amount of within-country variation in the scope of asset portfolio diversification among elites. For an excellent micro-level analysis of how these patterns explain
differences in policy preferences and political strategies in Argentina and Chile throughout
the nineteenth and twentieth centuries, see Paniagua (2018). Our point is simply that levels of
cross-sector/industry ownership in late industrializers is higher because early rural elites have a
prominent role in the design and implementation of the industrialization process that primarily
improves productivity in the rural economy (Haber, 2005).

and limited fiscal capacity, a situation elites try to protect by resisting democratization (Boix, 2003; Soifer, 2015). When democratization does occur, it is strongly shaped by rural elites to encourage conservative outcomes via malapportionment and limitations in suffrage (Albertus and Menaldo, 2014; Boone and Wahman, 2015).

Yet, clearly not all societies with powerful rural elites remained locked in a preindustrial world. Precisely because geography is not the only long-run determinant of labor costs, several factors may lead to a relative increase of rural labor costs over time, and through that to the demand for innovation and the expansion of the manufacturing sector. Haber (2005), for instance, illustrates how in Argentina, Brazil, and Mexico such demand emerged endogenously in the period 1870–1910 due to a combination of the currency attachment to the silver standard, the reduction of transportation costs, and the inflow of FDI to export-oriented sectors (mining, beef, coffee). Regardless of the specific transition mechanisms, the relevant political question is how rural elites adapt to a new scenario combining high (or at least growing) labor costs and economic concentration. Under these circumstances rural elites in late industrializing nations seek technological advancements and expansion of manufacturing in a process controlled by themselves. Through their influence in the political arena, rural elites adapt and expand their realm of activity into emerging industrial activities. And, as a result, observable outcomes reflect a compromise between the preferences, outlined earlier, of largely overlapping rural and industrial elites. The idea is to minimize the disruption of industrialization and ensure that the new areas of economic production remain functional for their core interests. Industrialization is largely a process heavily monitored, if not directly shaped, by rural elites. Unsurprisingly, they manage to keep their social and spatial advantages.

SPATIAL ECONOMIC CONCENTRATION: RAIL DEVELOPMENT IN ARGENTINA
Argentina was one of the first industrialized nations outside of Western Europe and the former British Colonies. The industrialization process began in the late 1800s with investments in mechanized agriculture to increase productivity in the primary export products of wheat and beef (Haber, 2005). These investments were made by agricultural elites in cooperation with British and, to a lesser extent, American and German capitalists to improve the export of these products for European consumption. At the same time, the Argentine government coordinated with foreign (mostly British and American) investors and companies to construct

railway lines to bring commodities to the port city of Buenos Aires for export to Europe and North America. Figure 8 shows the primarily British-constructed railway network in 1914, which shows a clear hub-and-spoke pattern oriented toward Buenos Aires. The high concentration of rail lines is in the province of Buenos Aires. The Patagonian South is not featured on the map because no lines ran to it.

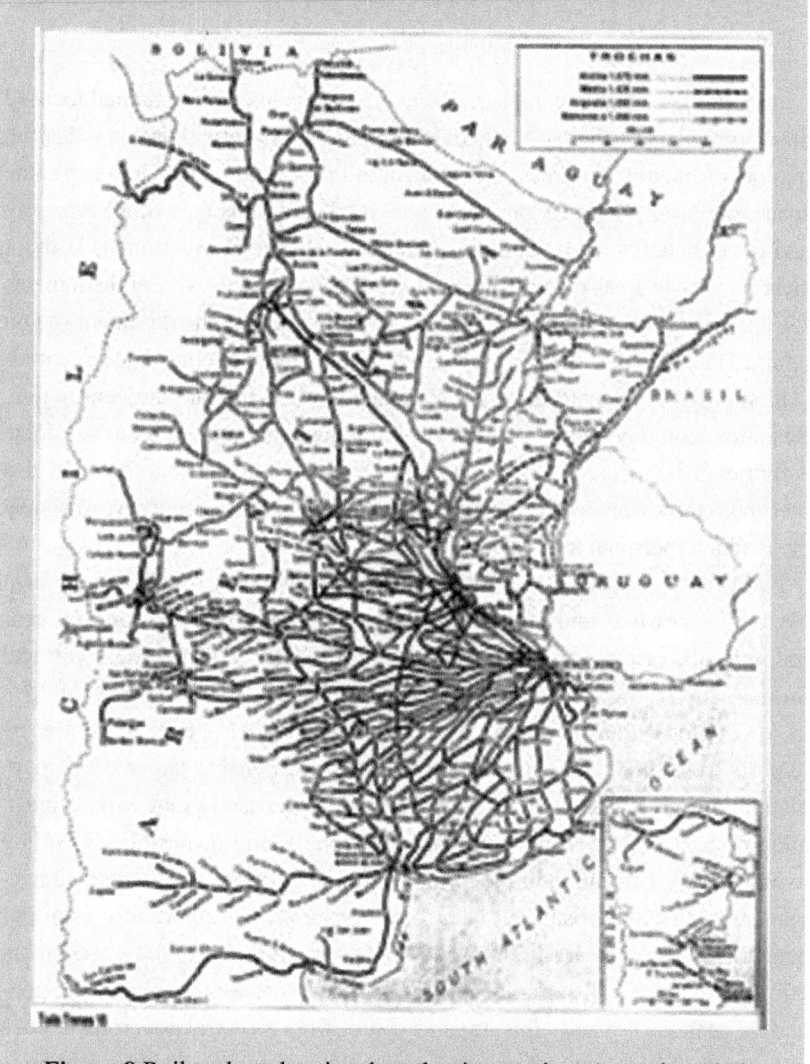

Figure 8 Railroads and national market integration: Argentina 1940.

In contrast to the UK and the North of the United States, we see an example of a fragmented national market in the case of Argentina. Argentina made weak efforts to incorporate the whole of the national territory into the national market. Rather, the entire rail network operated in a hub-and-spoke pattern radiating out only from metropolitan Buenos Aires. To this day, travel within the interior of Argentina is not possible by train, and is relatively slow through other forms of transportation. The large majority of transportation continues to go in and out via Buenos Aires.

Importantly, while late industrializers' economic interests remained focused on the products of the land, whether through export agriculture or industrial outputs of natural resources, the concentration of productivity in geographic space remained. The creation of national markets in this type of an economy had fewer benefits, and would have entailed substantial investments without clear payoffs in areas outside the most productive regions. Absent the impetus for improving the economic conditions of the periphery, the dominant region retained the bulk of economic productivity. Under these circumstances, centralization of fiscal capacity is very threatening to elites in that dominant region. Resources could be redistributed away from the dominant region to subsidize activities in the periphery. In addition, the centralization of resources could also be captured by workers in the increasingly industrialized economy, who may demand interpersonal transfers.

Failures of national market integration related to weak fiscal capacity help explain "excessive" and "suboptimal" concentration of population in a central, typically primate city in late industrializers (Henderson, 2002; Scott and Storper, 2003). The concentration of population is understood to be a function of lower global transportation costs, which allow urban needs to be met by imports from the countryside and abroad and thus enable larger urban populations (Puga, 1998). Venables (2005) and others also point to inefficient allocation of property rights and concentration of land ownership as leading to excessive urbanization in the primate city rather than more balanced development in first suburban, and later, other urban areas. Importantly from our perspective, the deconcentration of population requires explicit government efforts to increase transportation and infrastructure networks to alternative population centers. Typically this impetus comes from a central government keen to lower the high costs and negative externalities associated with overly large urban areas (Venables, 2005). Put in the perspective of our research, deconcentrating the primate city requires focused efforts at interregional redistribution and substantial, high-quality infrastructure investments, typically made by the central government. We have seen successful examples of this in Seoul, South

Korea, and to some extent China, but few other efforts in late developers (Choe et al., 1987; Chun and Lee, 1985). Thus, late developers maintain megacities despite high costs due to failures of interregional redistribution and lack of investments in public goods outside of the early developing region.

Perhaps the most important arenas of elite coordination in the central government are on the provision of public goods, and trade and monetary policies. In early industrializers, the expansion of public goods and push for trade openness came from industrial and capital elites eager to sell their products on the international market (Lindert, 2004). The transition to open markets and broader public goods provision happened once industrial elites increased their voice in a competitive decision-making process. Industrial elites in late industrializers, on the other hand, did not have the same demand for trade openness because they preferred high tariffs to grow their industries. They did not demand the same levels of public goods because their economies remained more agricultural (and thus less in need of public goods investments) than early industrializers. Accordingly, as we elaborate in detail in Section 4.3, late industrializers never pressed for the expansion of fiscal capacity seen in early industrializers (Beramendi et al., 2018). Incomplete and late trade openness is associated with the perpetuation of uneven regional fortunes. Openness to trade is a very strong predictor of low geographic concentration. Henderson (2002, p. 100) finds, "International trade also affects primate city size: a one-standard-deviation increase (48.8) in openness (imports plus exports as a percent of GDP) decreases primate city size by 27 percent." The new economic geography models also predict that a country's exposure to trade may encourage hinterland development in recent phases of development (Krugman and Elizondo, 1996; Krugman and Venables, 1995; Puga and Venables, 1996).

4.3 Late Industrializers with Low Dispersion

Some late industrializers did not encounter such significant problems of uneven economic endowments and a dominant agricultural elite in their industrial transition. In those cases the challenge was in the initial industrialization decision, to find a way to prosper given existing competition from early industrializers. The nations that fit this category tend to have more even economic endowments and have fortunate locations from a trading or geopolitical perspective. We focus on Scandinavian nations and South Korea as emblematic of this experience. It should be noted that a number of low-dispersion countries, including the smaller nations in Latin America, never initiated substantial industrialization projects. In part, this was due to their relatively low levels of development and small internal markets. At least in the Latin American cases, the small

Political Economy

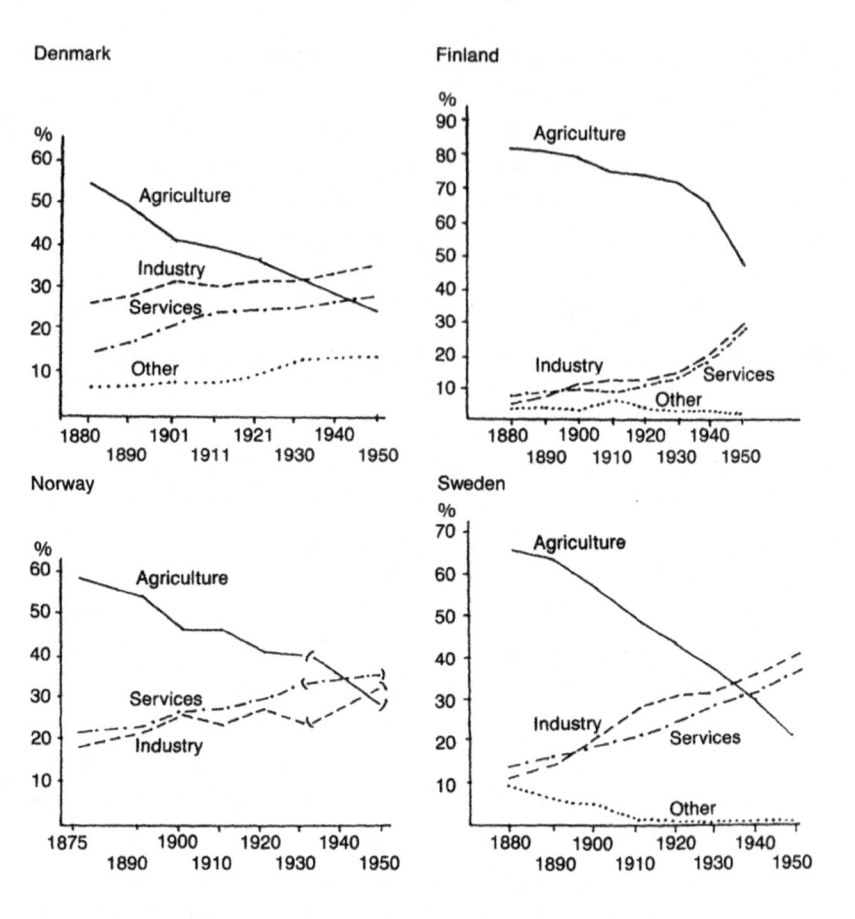

Figure 9 Late industrialization in Scandinavia.

Sectoral distribution of the economically active population in the Scandinavian countries, 1880–1950. *Source*: Alestalo and Kuhnle (1986).

nations could not expect to absorb industrial production within their nations and were late late industrializers – they faced competition not just from the early industrializers but also from their larger regional neighbors that industrialized in the mid-twentieth century.

Figure 9 shows the later industrializing pattern in Scandinavia. Denmark and Sweden industrialized earlier (1930s) than Norway (mid-1940s) or Finland (post-1950). In all cases, these nations industrialized after Britain and Central Europe. Scandinavia was the European periphery, and it traditionally exported to more-developed European nations. Denmark, Norway, and Sweden have been classified together with such countries as Argentina as predominantly agrarian countries with rapid primary export expansion, modest industrial development toward domestic markets, and rising per capita incomes in the early 1900s (Morris and Adelman, 1980). They also had in common the export to early industrializers, in this case the Netherlands and the United Kingdom, and later Germany. Finland was much further behind.

The industrialization process in Finland was much like that seen in late developers such as Argentina. The state intervened to modernize agriculture and the rural landowning elite invested in the mechanization of agriculture like in other late industrializers (Østerud, 1978). Finland's main agricultural export was timber (Alapuro, 1981). Industrialization was around the mechanization and increased productivity in the timber industry for the export of wood to Western Europe and paper products to Russia. In Scandinavia, like in other late industrializers, rural elites became increasingly urban and were highly involved with the state. They were the main source of recruitment as state bureaucrats and as military officers (Castles, 1973).

In cases such as Finland, the natural economic endowments, in terms of agricultural production or access to trading routes, were never substantial in any part of the country. Finland was not endowed with natural resources that made it able to compete in agricultural production with Europe, much less the highly productive US and Latin American agricultural exporters. Accordingly, Finland did not have a powerful status quo–oriented agricultural elite that could successfully block public goods investments. Instead, most agricultural production throughout Scandinavia came from individual proprietors, with small holdings (Alestalo and Kuhnle, 1986). Moreover, there was not a clear regional economic cleavage whereby economic elites in a dominant region fought centralization to avoid redistribution outward to the periphery. The primarily challenge to transition to industrial production in Finland was in the accumulation of capital to fund investments. In this case, as in most late industrializers, proceeds from timber paid for the capital to modernize agriculture and industrialize (Soininen, 1974).

The absence of clear regional cleavages is also apparent in Finland's urban and spatial development. Scandinavian nations did not have the same level of urban problems – slums and exploitation of labor – experienced in early developers or uneven late developers. The bulk of the social problems existed in rural areas, which manifest themselves in national politics and were later alleviated with democratic development and large welfare states (Kuhnle, 2013). Accordingly, we see spatial inequality falling with industrialization in Scandinavia, much like the early industrializers. Figure 11 shows Finland and Sweden's regional inequality falling fast with the rise of the industrial sector. We argue that the relative absence of spatial tensions made the centralization possible that enabled the welfare state to blossom in Scandinavia.

South Korea, a country with low dispersion and weak agricultural endowments, ultimately ended up on a similar path as the Scandinavian nations with regard to spatial inequalities. The destruction of the landed elite and class-based politics in South Korea enabled industrialization without a strong rural-based upper class that brought about regionalism in most other late developers. While conditions in South Korea were similar to many late developers, such as foreign investments in infrastructure (electricity, public transit, water) and foreign capital, the status quo–oriented agricultural elite and the agricultural–industrial linkages to that primate city were not present. The result has been economic expansion that, in the medium to long term, has spread out over the nation and has not resulted in substantial regional political cleavages.

Both South Korea and Finland industrialized in part for geopolitical strategic reasons, with investments from countries with geopolitical interests. Sweden, Norway, and Finland had the benefits of proximity to large markets in Western Europe. These factors may enhance the possibility of a "way out" from the regionalized, uneven development pattern of late industrializers, a theme we discuss in detail in volume II.

SPATIAL ECONOMIC DIFFUSION: NIGHTLIGHT
DECONCENTRATION IN SOUTH KOREA

South Korea has made significant efforts in the last twenty years to spread productivity across the nation (Evans, 2012). As Seoul has become very crowded and expensive, the central government has invested in transportation linkages to the suburbs and, more recently, expanding urban areas outside of the Seoul metro area.

Indeed, efforts at effective interregional redistribution, such as the efficient deconcentration of Seoul into multiple cities throughout the nation, were made possible by government provision of distributed infrastructure and education investments. Although the deconcentration of other primate cities in late developers might be similarly economically efficient, they have not been undertaken due to (endogenous) limitations in fiscal capacity and the desire to avoid truly effective interregional redistribution that may reduce the returns for elites in the richest regions in the country.

South Korea industrialized in the last half of the twentieth century. Given changes in transportation technology and the physical size of the nation, a direct comparison of the railroad network is not a compelling way to tell the story of South Korea's spatial diffusion. Instead, we focus in Figure 10 on the spatial distribution of nighttime brightness over the period of its greatest advances in development, 1992–2013. The spatial concentration of nighttime brightness (a proxy for productivity) declined dramatically in the period.

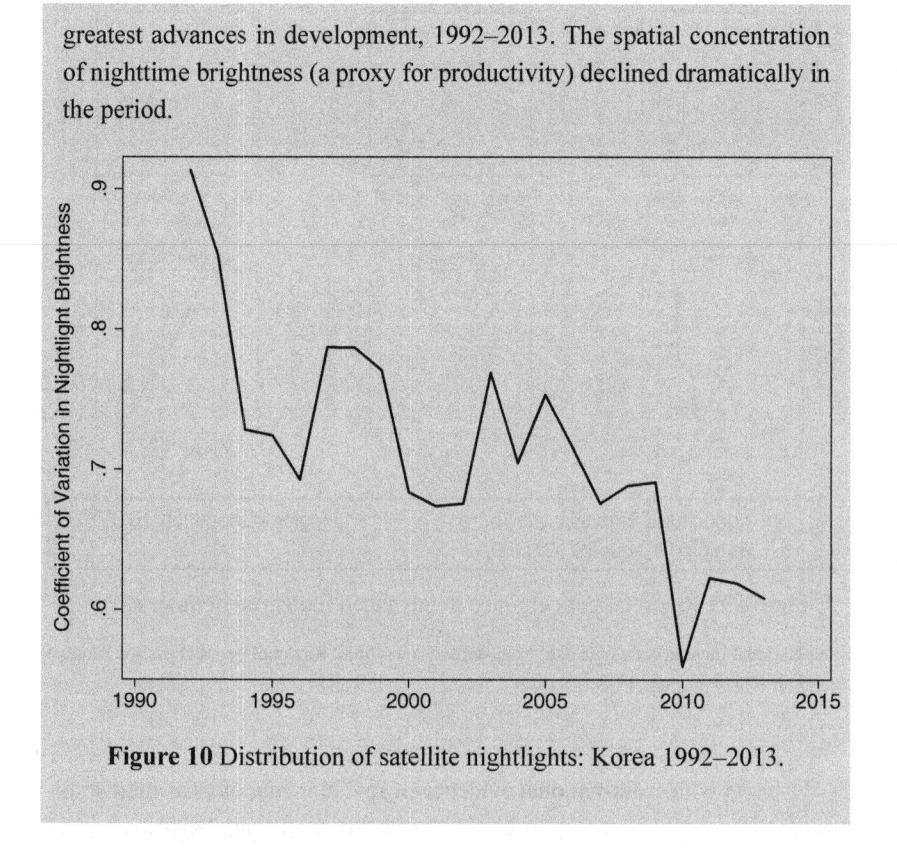

Figure 10 Distribution of satellite nightlights: Korea 1992–2013.

To summarize, in late industrializers, despite significant variation among them:

1. Commodity-based elites initiate industrialization to increase productivity in the primary sector, thus exacerbating the polarizing effect of natural geographic endowments.
2. Due to differences in technology, the subnational regions with the most valuable natural endowments feed into megacities fueled by both primary sector and industrial production.
3. The exceptions to the process are few but include those with favorable access to early industrializers' markets (e.g., Scandinavia) or important geopolitical positions (e.g., South Korea).

5 Spatial Trends in Development: Evidence from GNI and GDP Distributions

In the following sections, we bring data to our accounts of spatial inequalities in early and late industrializers (hypothesis 1), and the fate of spatial inequalities during and as a result of the industrialization process (hypothesis

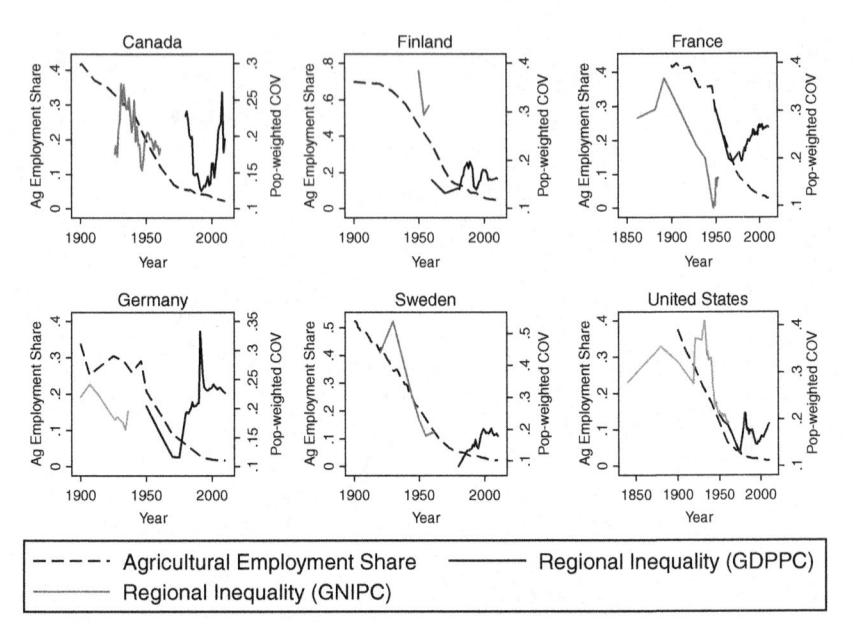

Figure 11 Regional convergence in advanced industrial democracies.

Gross National Income per capita data from Williamson (1965). Regional Gross Domestic Product per capita data from Rogers (2015).

2). We begin with cross-national evidence of spatial inequalities as industrialization progressed around the world. Comparable data on spatial distributions of productivity and income are not easy to come by in the current period, much less historically. We take the best available historical data on subnational distributions (coefficients of variation) in Gross National Income (GNI) per capita from Williamson (1965), collected in the 1960s, and compare them with our more recent data on distributions of subnational GDP per capita for all nations with available data. We plot the evolution of subnational distributions of production in comparison to national data on the share of agricultural employment in the economy. The agricultural share of the economy data provides a rough indicator of where that country is in its stage of industrial development, or at least its movement away from employment in the primary economy. Thus, we can compare countries at similar stages, rather than fully industrialized or postindustrial levels to countries still in their industrial transition.

We begin with data from some early industrializing countries: France, USA, Canada, and Germany, as well as some on the later end, Sweden and Finland, in Figure 11. In each nation, we can see the fairly steep evolution away from agricultural employment, in some cases earlier than 1900 (Germany, France, USA, Canada) and in some cases primarily in the twentieth century (Finland,

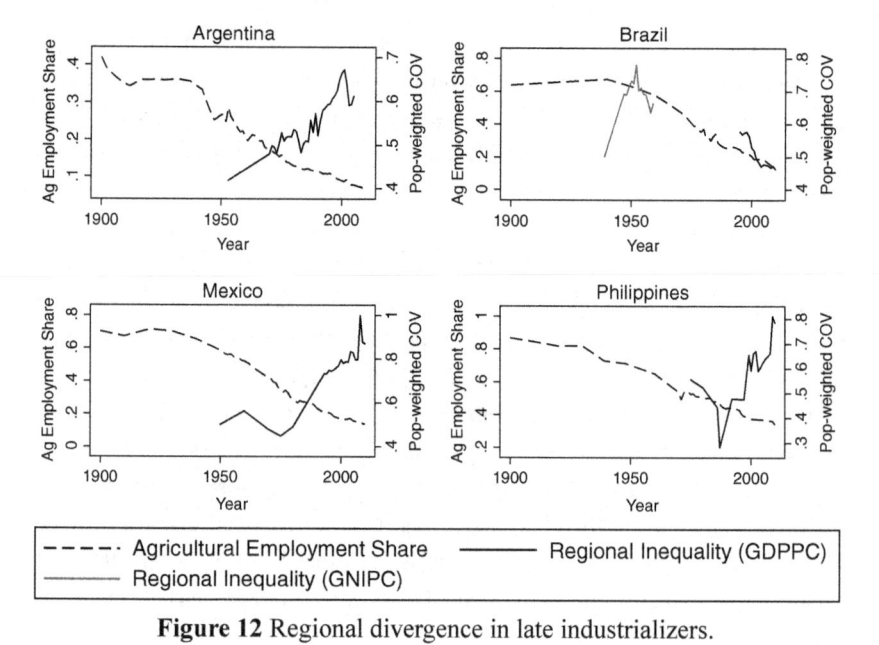

Figure 12 Regional divergence in late industrializers.

Gross National Income per capita data from Williamson (1965). Regional Gross Domestic Product per capita data from Rogers (2015).

Sweden). Piecing together the subnational distributions in GNI per capita and GDP per capita, we can see significant reductions in the extent of regional inequality in productivity in the twentieth century. The cases of Sweden and Finland are illustrative. Sweden starts the twentieth century with approximately 60 percent agricultural employment. At that time, subnational inequality in GNI was high by continental standards (approximately .5) but not high by global standards in the period or by global standards in the modern era, as we shall see in the next charts. In both Sweden and Finland, the decline in agricultural employment coincides with regional convergence in GNI, and later GDP per capita. By the end of the twentieth century, both nations have very low coefficients of variation in regional productivity, among the lowest in the world. This convergence, as is apparent in the historical data, emerged prior to the consolidation of national welfare states in the postwar periods. We see similar trends in France, the USA, and Canada, with regional convergence flowing through the period of industrialization, ending up with very low regional disparities in production by the modern era.

Figure 12 provides comparable evidence for late industrializing nations: Brazil, Mexico, Argentina, and the Philippines. Not surprisingly, data availability is sparser in the late developing nations. Williamson (1965) only has historical GNI evidence for Brazil. Our regional GDP per capita estimates for Mexico, Argentina, and India span back to the 1950s, however, allowing some comparability at the level of agricultural employment with early industrializing nations. For example, Argentina in the 1950s had agricultural employment of around 40 percent, or comparable levels to Sweden in the 1920s or Finland in the 1940s. Brazil and Mexico reach 40 percent agricultural employment share in the 1960s. The Philippines reached 40 percent agricultural employment share in the 1990s. A first observation of these data should be the scale of the second y-axis in comparison to the early industrializers. The late industrializers have regional coefficients of variation of between .5 and 1. The peak values in the twentieth century in the early industrializers were between .4 and .5. Indeed, the late industrializers mostly start at similar levels of distribution, around .4–.5, but rise to .7 or more (close to 1 in the case of Mexico) as industrialization progresses. Brazil's regional disparities have fallen since their peak in the 1950s, but their current level (approximately .5) remains double that of the most unequal early industrializing case (France) in Figure 11.

What should be apparent from all four cases featured in this figure is that regional convergence is not apparent in the data for late industrializers (Henderson, 2002; Venables, 2005). At the point we can document relative convergence in the early industrializers, we see the late industrializers increasingly diverge in regional GDP per capita terms. At the flux point in the early industrializers, around 40 percent of agricultural employment, we see a spike in regional inequality in Mexico, Argentina, and the Philippines. Brazil shows a similar spike in the 50 percent agricultural employment range that has been largely maintained into the current period. We attribute this regional divergence or at least persistent regional inequality to limitations in the process of national market integration and, subsequently, to limited redistribution to individuals and regions, all traceable to weakness in fiscal capacity and persistent regional-based conflicts over centralized distributive policies. This latter link is the focus of Volume II.

The patterns of regional divergence in late developers documented in Figure 12 are not the only possible paths for late developers. The case of South Korea, mentioned earlier, is one in which industrial elites interested in human capital development pursued that development under an autocratic regime. As discussed earlier, that autocracy essentially eliminated the agricultural elite in that nation, cutting off the entrenched land-based interests. Early agglomeration in Seoul has since the 1970s been distributed with increasing regularity throughout the space of that nation. The endpoint of this process is apparent in the upper right panel of Figure 13. Unfortunately we do not have data prior to 1990, but

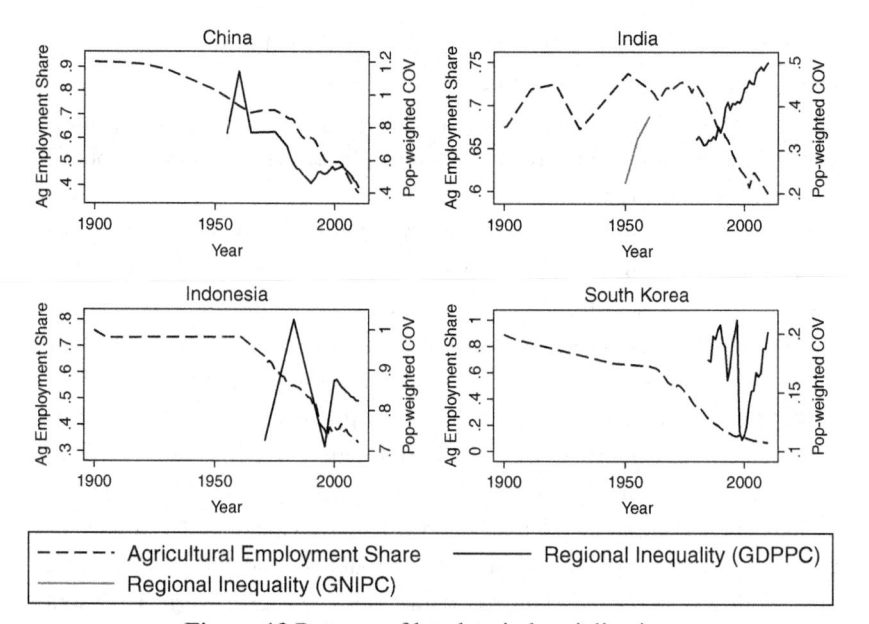

Figure 13 Patterns of late late industrialization.

Gross National Income per capita data from Williamson (1965). Regional Gross Domestic Product per capita data from Rogers (2015).

what we see at 1990 is a low level of regional inequality in comparative perspective (at or less than .2). South Korea has regional convergence comparable with the early industrializers.

China is also an interesting case of regional development in late industrialization. While regional inequality in China is notoriously high (Jian et al., 1996; Kanbur and Zhang, 2005), it appears to have fallen with industrial deepening. From its peak of a coefficient of variation of nearly 1.2, China's regional inequality has fallen to levels comparable with Latin America between the 1960s and 1990s. Like with South Korea, China's agricultural elite was largely eliminated in the twentieth century. Enormous agglomeration in only a few cities on the coast have started to expand into more cities to reduce environmental and infrastructural strain. China's "One Belt, One Road" policy to link the nation in a common, integrated infrastructure represents serious efforts to distribute productivity and development throughout the nation.

The convergence trends seen in China and South Korea are not yet apparent in the industrialization processes of India and Indonesia in Figure 13. The verdict may still be out on India, which has not reached 50 percent nonagricultural employment. Rather, agricultural employment remained rather stagnant in the twentieth century. Meanwhile, regional divergence in GDP per capita is growing from levels akin to the early developers in the 1980s to levels similar to Latin America in 2010.[19] Indonesia has reached the approximate point at which we might expect regional convergence or divergence to emerge, but it has hovered around a high coefficient of variation of around .8 from the 1970s to the present.

We do not have subnational GDP and population data to account for spatial inequalities in most of sub-Saharan Africa. This is unfortunate because there are good reasons to believe that this global region struggles most with both the levels of and political implications of spatial inequalities. While precolonial spatial inequality in sub-Saharan Africa may have been low, due to limited economic development and differentiation, the colonial period created and exacerbated differences (Bigsten, 2016). Colonial infrastructure investments in areas with the most profitable agriculture and resources (especially mining) made these regions pull far ahead of the undeveloped regions. Boone (2003) argues that these uneven territorial investments are a product of state-building, in which areas with few economic endowments are not considered worth incorporating into the state. Boone and Simson (2019) argue that spatial divisions in the region were created in many cases to lock in existing patterns of distribution and ethnic divides. Moreover, the beginnings of industrialization that came to sub-Saharan Africa may have further exacerbated spatial inequalities, as the cities that had been pushed ahead in the colonial period gained the bulk of the benefits from employment, industrial subsidies, and infrastructure (Bates, 2005).

In Figure 14 we put forward our best available evidence on subnational inequalities in sub-Saharan Africa. We plot the coefficient of variation in subnational nightlight brightness for a selected sample of sub-Saharan African nations in comparison with selected Latin American nations, the region identified as having the highest spatial inequalities in GDP per capita data (Rogers, 2016). The black lines represent subnational variation in 1992; the gray lines show subnational variation in 2013. While Latin America's values are high, especially Peru, the sub-Saharan values are higher, in some cases much higher. For example, Mali, the Central African Republic, Ethiopia, and Uganda have levels of spatial inequality that are upwards of three times worse than the average values in Latin America. Much more needs to be understood about the contributions of colonial legacies, commodities production, and nascent industrialization at a time of very low transportation costs in sub-Saharan Africa (Boone and Simson, 2019). One of the strong legacies of colonialism in sub-Saharan Africa, for example, is extreme restrictions on population mobility that

---

[19] See Lee (2019) on variation in public goods provision across states in India.

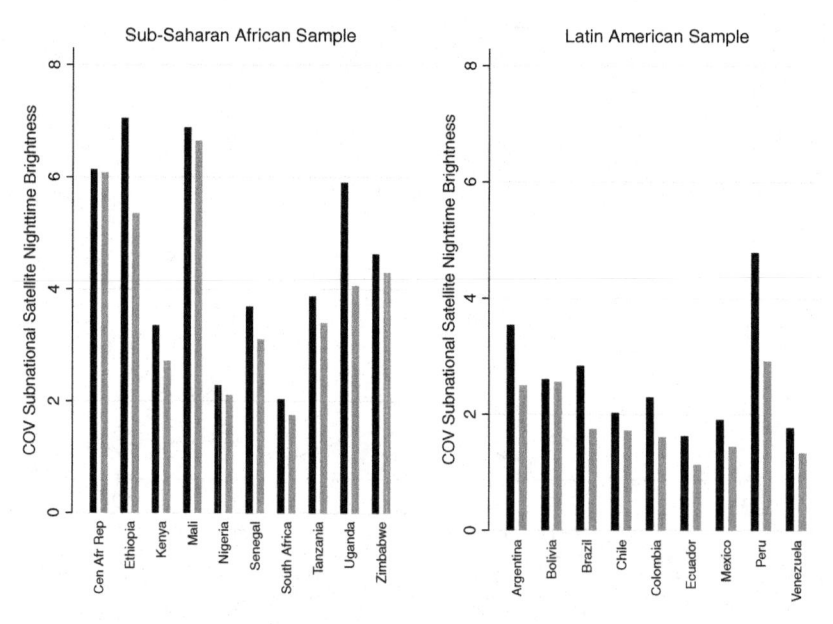

Figure 14 Subnational nightlight variation in sub-Saharan Africa and Latin America.

Black lines are values from 1992, gray lines are values from 2013. *Source*: Authors' calculation from the DMSP OLS: Global Radiance-Calibrated Nighttime Lights Version 4, Defense Meteorological Program Operational Linescan System.

severely hampers labor markets (Adebusoye et al., 2006; Van Dijk et al., 2001). This region may have the most extreme circumstances from the standpoint of our theory, likely contributing to the strong regionalism in politics and conflict over centralization.

The challenge in examining countries at different levels of development in our analysis is to define (and find) relevant comparisons. In the case of the early developers, we often do not have reasonable historical data to match the values for late industrializers. Even those countries that we consider late developers, such as Argentina or Brazil, industrialized prior to the period of wide data availability for values such as regional productivity. In Figure 15 we do our best to provide an "apples to apples" comparison of regional convergence processes for nations currently at different levels of industrialization. We take the four cases for which we have data farthest back in the industrialization process, when agricultural employment dropped below 40 percent of total employment, and plot their trends from that point. The *y*-axis plots the count of years since that country dropped below 40 percent agricultural employment. The early industrializing mixed case, the USA, starts at levels of regional inequality that

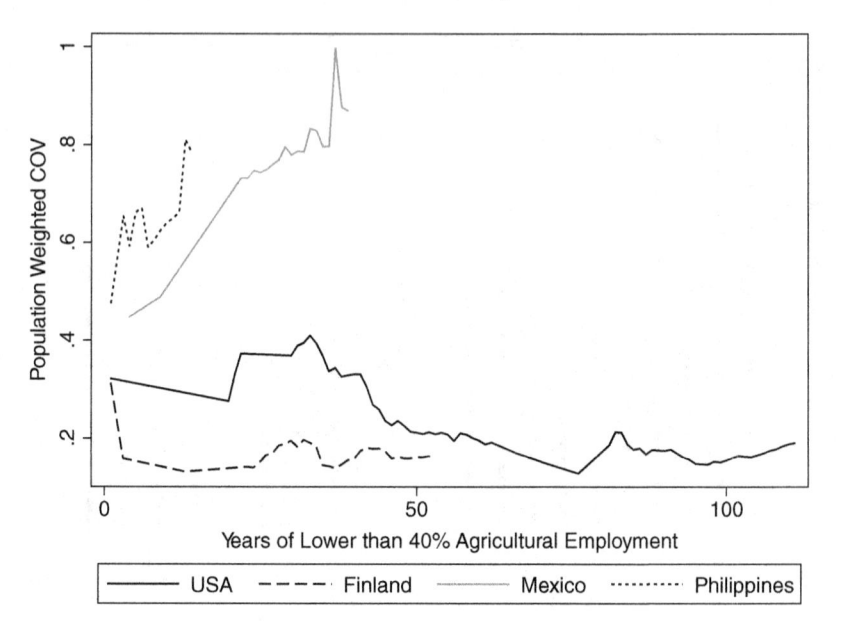

Figure 15 Regional distribution as industrialization progresses.

Gross National Income per capita data used prior to 1950 in USA and prior to 1970 for Finland, from Williamson (1965). Regional Gross Domestic Product per capita data from Rogers (2015).

are not unlike those seen in late developing nations, with coefficients of variation higher than .35. Indeed, this value appears to be the rough starting point for the late developing nations prior to industrial deepening. From a similar approximate starting point, the USA and Finland (a low-dispersion late industrializer) see a broad decline in regional inequality in productivity into a low steady state. The USA's process was slower and bumpier than Finland's. The trend is quite different for high-dispersion late industrializers. Both Mexico and the Philippines see strong upward trends and persistent high levels of regional divergence with industrial deepening. While these trends may one day reverse themselves, we did not see similar trends in the early industrializers or low-dispersion late industrializers, and the levels of regional inequality are much higher than those ever seen in early industrializers for periods for which we have data. This chart supports claims by Henderson (2002) and Venables (2005), among others, who document the absence of regional convergence in late developers.

5.1 Analysis: Geography, Industrialization, and Spatial Inequality

The previous sections have provided descriptive evidence of divergence between early and late industrializers in their spatial distribution of economic productivity, focusing especially on hypothesis 1. In this section we test whether these differences are driven solely by geography, or by the interaction of the spatial distribution of endowments and productivity and the timing of industrialization, as we argue in hypothesis 2.

We provide evidence consistent with this dynamic in Figure 16. We plot the association between variation in subnational economic endowments on the x-axis and uneven subnational economic productivity on the y-axis in early and late industrializers. In the panel showing early industrializers, we see almost no relationship between the coefficient of variation in subnational economic endowments and the coefficient of variation in subnational GDP per capita. The countries with high variation in subnational GDP per capita are not necessarily those with disparate geography. Disparate geography, as in the cases of Australia, Canada, or Norway, does not automatically translate into uneven economic productivity across the nation. We suggest this is due to investments made at the time of industrialization in regions throughout the nation and the free movement of people made possible by those infrastructure investments and the gains from industrialization. The relative equality of regions has persisted in the long term due to these investments, and due to redistributive policies that spread resources throughout the nation (more on this in volume II).

The relationship between variation in economic endowments and variation in subnational productivity is much stronger in late industrializing nations. In these nations, high variation in economic endowments is associated with high subnational disparities in economic productivity. Moreover, it is useful to consider the difference in scale in the subnational inequality measure in Figure 16. Consistent with hypothesis 1, we see far higher subnational economic disparities in late developing nations. Regional inequality peaks at around .37 in the early industrializing sample (Czech Republic), while it is over 3.6 times larger in the highest regional inequality nation in Figure 16(b), Ecuador. It is precisely these interregional inequalities that we argue will heighten elite tensions over redistribution that ultimately lead to underinvestment in the capacity of the central state.

We demonstrate the same dynamic using regression analysis. In our estimates we include parsimonious, standard controls discussed in Section 3.4, including GDP per capita, partisanship of the chief executive, and experience with major interstate war. Consistent with hypothesis 2, we expect to see that the link between economic endowments and long-run spatial inequalities is different between early and late industrializers. In early industrializers, we should see at best a weak connection between distributions of natural economic endowments and economic productivity at the regional level. In late industrializers the connection between the two should be robust, as late

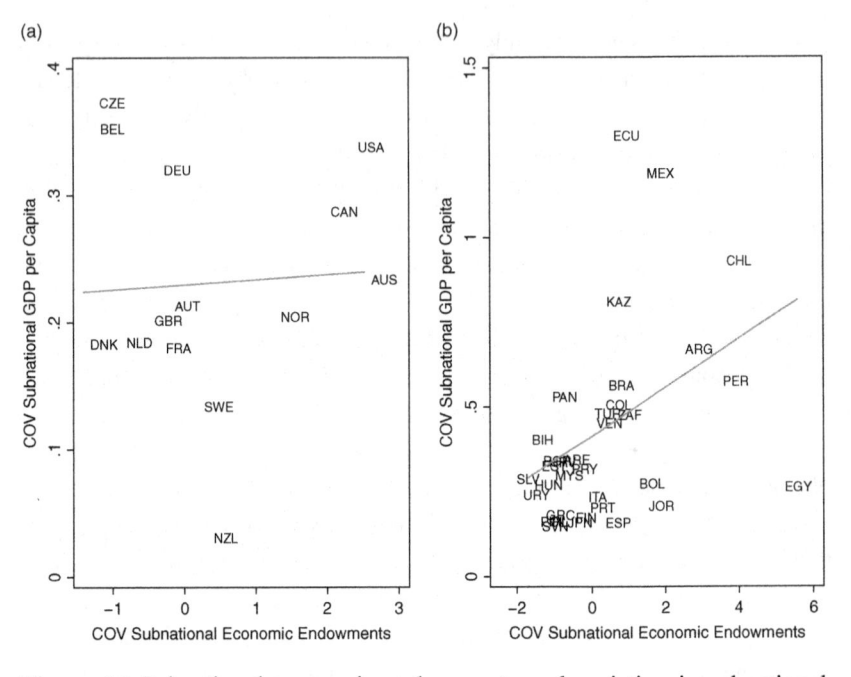

Figure 16 Subnational economic endowments and variation in subnational productivity.

Cross-sectional data of national mean values. Variables: Coefficients of variation in subnational economic endowments (agricultural suitability and access to trade), coefficient of variation in subnational GDP per capita (Rogers, 2016). Countries with higher than 30 percent agricultural employment in 2010 excluded.

industrialization does not alleviate spatial inequalities, but in many cases compounds them.

Figure 17 plots the average marginal effects of the interaction term between the timing of industrialization and subnational variation in economic endowments.[20] In Figure 17(a), the dependent variable is the coefficient of variation in subnational GDP per capita. In Figure 17(b), the dependent variable is the Gini coefficient of subnational GDP per capita. The figure shows clearly that in early industrializers there is not a strong link between variation in subnational endowments and subnational economic productivity in the long term. In late industrializers, the link between endowments and productivity outcomes is strong and positive. This suggests that the underlying economic geography is a much stronger predictor of long-term productivity in late industrializers than early industrializers. Indeed, in early industrializers, there is

---

[20] Full results in Appendix 2.1.

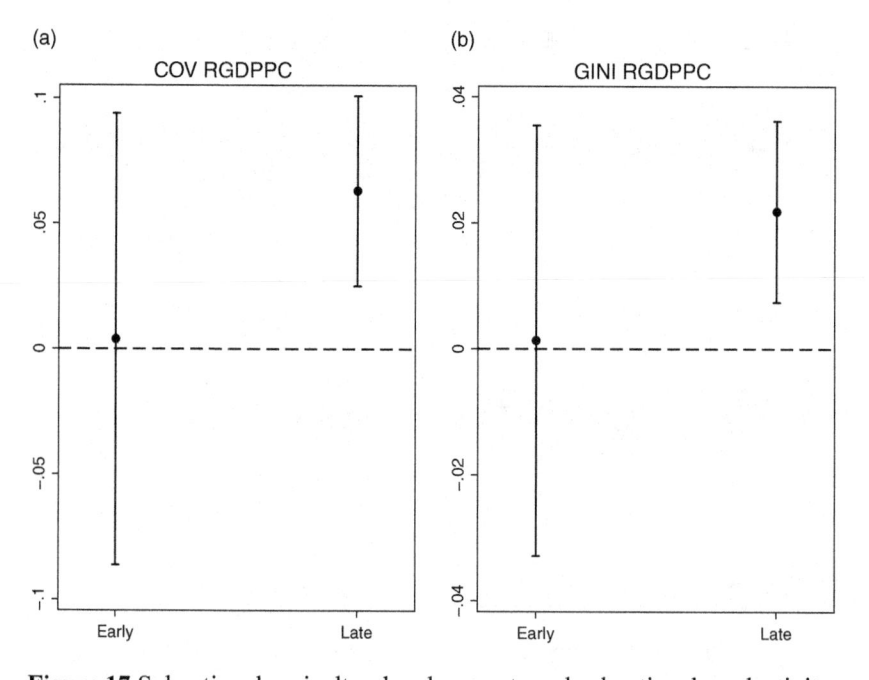

Figure 17 Subnational agricultural endowments and subnational productivity, regression analysis.

Cross-sectional data of national mean values. Independent variable: coefficient of variation in subnational economic endowments. Dependent variables: coefficient of variation in subnational GDP per capita (Rogers, 2016); region-adjusted Gini coefficient in subnational GDP per capita (Rogers, 2016).

no discernible relationship between variation in underlying economic endowments and variation in subnational productivity. As shown in the Appendix, this result is not sensitive to the measure of regional inequality, the choice of geographic unit, the date distinguishing early and late industrialization, or the sample.

6 Political Implications of Spatial Development

Our analysis so far has centered around documenting the interaction between economic geography and the patterns of industrialization. We have shown that phases of industrialization interact with preexisting economic geography in fundamentally different ways. Early industrializers tend to build integrated domestic markets through dense networks of infrastructure that facilitate the circulation of both labor and manufacturers. The result is a relative spatial spread of prosperity, a network in which multiple centers of production, distribution, and consumption are clustered in urban space and connected by a

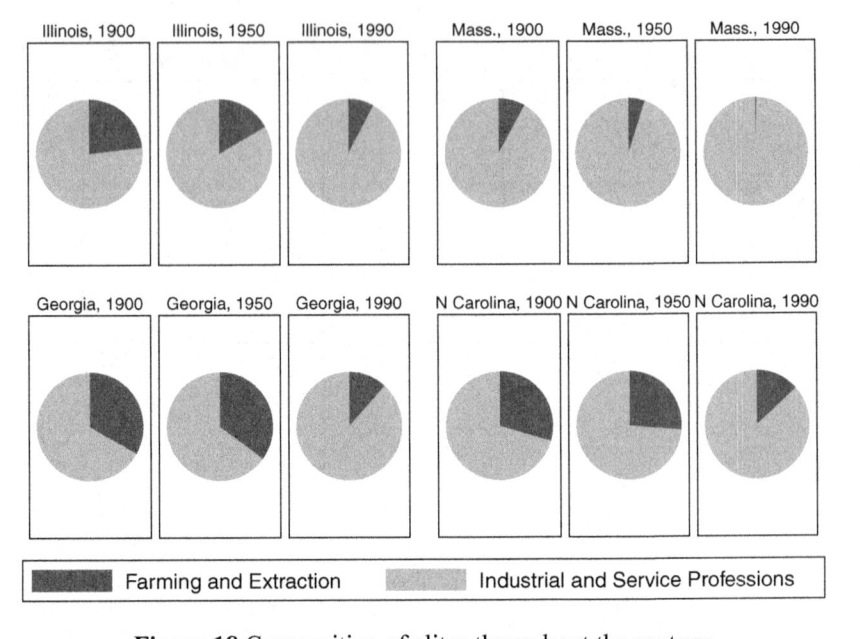

Illinois, 1900   Illinois, 1950   Illinois, 1990   Mass., 1900   Mass., 1950   Mass., 1990

Georgia, 1900   Georgia, 1950   Georgia, 1990   N Carolina, 1900   N Carolina, 1950   N Carolina, 1990

Farming and Extraction   Industrial and Service Professions

Figure 18 Composition of elites throughout the century.

Data on employment of state legislators. Farming and Extraction careers are primary-sector-based careers. Industry and Service sector careers are those in the secondary and tertiary sectors (business, finance, legal, education, health) (Beramendi et al., 2021).

transportation network. As a result, geographic economic differences become less stark a determinant of the patterns of long-run prosperity. By contrast, in late industrializers a more polarized economic geography to begin with limits the incentives and the capacity to develop integrated national markets. Elites concentrate efforts and investments in specific locations for either extraction and distribution and refrain from pursuing integrated national markets to the same extent. As a result, economic modernization further reinforces spatial polarization.

We turn now to discuss the political implications of these processes and one important channel through which they are bound to have long-lasting political effects: the composition of economic and political elites and their territorial distribution. The distribution of elites in space matters because it determines the expected preferences for fiscal development within and between areas. In early industrializing areas we should observe higher levels of elite heterogeneity at first. Industrialization triggers a major shock in social structures. At the bottom, the large-scale population displacement from rural areas into urban centers radically alters the distribution of income (Kuznets, 1955). At the top, the incumbent land aristocracy, whose wealth and power relies on the exploitation of land, sees its dominance increasingly challenged by manufacturers and traders. Obviously, the existence of these groups predates industrialization. It is their social and economic leverage that grows exponentially with it. The resulting tension, anticipated by Adam Smith and more starkly captured by David Ricardo and Karl Marx, grows in intensity as industrialization progresses.

We examine elite composition in a mixed case, the USA, where early industrialization occurred in the Northeast, but the South remained primarily agricultural until after World War II. We expect to see a different composition of elites in these areas, with different demands for public goods investments.

Figure 18 provides a detailed picture of the change over time in the composition of elites across four US states: Massachusetts, Illinois, Georgia, and North Carolina. The figure depicts the relative share of two types of legislators: those with direct economic interests in farming and mining (primary sector, with dark gray segments) and those with direct ties to industry and service-related professions (light gray segments). The latter include occupations in both secondary and tertiary sectors. The figure starts in 1900, a moment in which industrialization is well underway in the Northeast and the Midwest, but nowhere else.

Early in the period, the relative presence of representatives with direct interests in the industrial and service sectors is much higher in Illinois and Massachusetts than in Georgia or North Carolina. As the process of economic modernization unfolds, the representation of the agricultural economy declines everywhere but at a much lower pace and from a much higher level in late industrializing areas. These differential dynamics are displayed more clearly in Figure 19. It displays the share of nonfarming occupations among members of the state legislature. Elite selection drives the concentration of preferences. In areas like Illinois and Massachusetts, or more broadly, any early industrializer, we see a rapid decline in the share of representatives whose preferences would be to limit the scope of pro-industrialization investments. By contrast, in states whose industrialization reflects more the input of export-oriented large landowners (e.g., cotton in Georgia or tobacco in North Carolina) we see much more limited support for investments.

Even with the capitalization of farming, we are not likely to see agriculture elites develop strong preferences for state capacity and the provision of public goods. Dasgupta (2020), writing in the context of US states in the mid-twentieth century, shows that farmers increasingly supported low taxation and public goods as they became more heavily capitalized due to changes in irrigation technology. Those farmers that were able to expand production

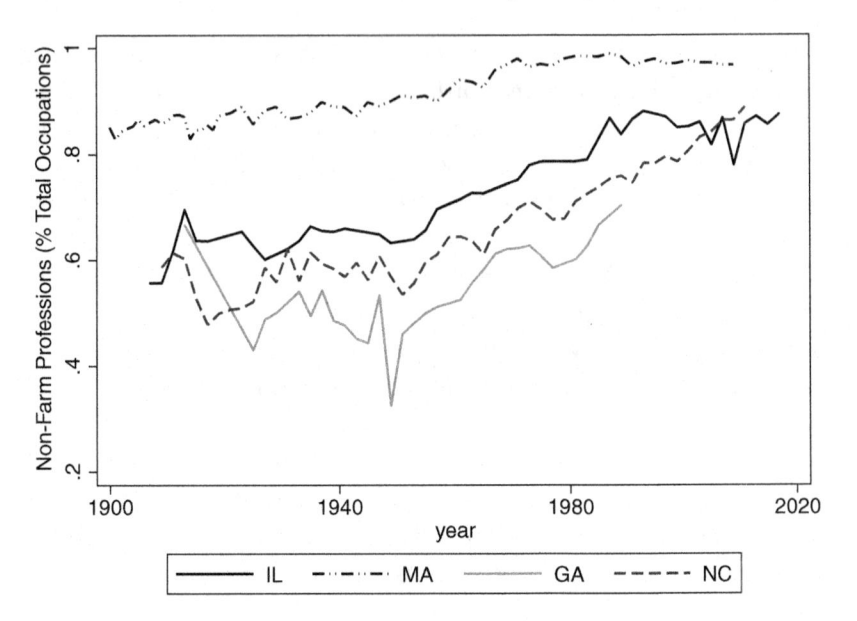

Figure 19 Transformation of elite linkage away from farming: US states 1900–2020.

States: IL (Illinois), MA (Massachusetts), GA (Georgia), NC (North Carolina). Data on employment of state legislators in Non-Farming Professions. Farming and Extraction careers are primary-sector-based careers. (Beramendi et al., 2021).

due to investments in these new technologies increasingly supported small government policy positions and conservative economic parties. As agriculture becomes more productive due to industrialization and technological investment, agriculture elites are likely to hold increasingly anti-state capacity positions.

The US case helps to demonstrate the compounding impact of industrialization on existing spatial divides. Where the agriculture economy was industrialized, as we argued was the case for late industrializers and mixed cases, the capitalization of farmers is a form of elite homogeneity. As the farmers became industrialists invested in the mechanization of the primary sector, they remained opposed to increasing state capacity. Indeed they may have taken even stronger opposition to state capacity investments, as shown in the US case. Capitalized farmers did not have the preferences for public goods provision that motivated industrialists to support stronger state capacity to fund infrastructure and health and education improvements for the workforce.

As argued earlier, the spatial variation in the pace and density of the development of the railroad network, for both freights and people, illustrates these process. Railroads reduce transportation costs relative to water lines, facilitate the development and integration of urban centers, thus integrating markets for goods and services, and enable relatively larger labor pools around production centers. They also help connect production and distribution centers for agricultural commodities and manufactures. We saw this divergence in the early railroad networks in the United States in Figure 7 in Section 4. In the Northeast and the Midwest, railroads grew earlier, faster, and more densely. In the Southeast, efforts to develop railways were more restricted to the circulation and treatment of agricultural commodities, and only later caught up somewhat with the rest of the union. There remains, however, a significant anchoring effect in the profile of the railroad network across regions that remains visible even in current times.

This anchoring effect of the initial logic of economic and political modernization, which in political terms we proxy with the occupational composition of the state legislature, is not constrained to the development of railways. Our argument is that it has an important, gripping impact on the development of the fiscal state and the nature of redistributive politics around the world. The impact is visible even in the United States and even in the aftermath of the big push toward fiscal centralization that followed the two World Wars.

The Sixteenth Amendment in 1913 and the Revenue Act of 1918 mark the introduction of tools that became widely used and effective at raising revenues only after 1942. Withholding for wage earners was introduced in 1943, and tax deductions for income earners in 1944. Critically, the IRS replaced the patronage system of personnel selection for career staffers in 1952, under President Truman. It is in this period when the features of a modern tax system become recognizable and the revenue generation capacity truly takes off. During this time, states join the federal government in the re-organization of their own tax systems.

Figure 20 maps the composition of state taxes in the four cases selected for our running example. In Figure 20(a) we show the rise of total tax revenue from all sources, per capita. In Figure 20(b) we show revenue from taxes on individual and corporate income. All four share a significant increase in the taxes collected after 1950, yet they diverge in their size and internal composition. At the extremes, Massachusetts and Georgia exemplify how early versus late industrializers vary in the internal organization of their tax systems. Massachusetts grows faster on the basis of a larger expansion of income taxes at the expense of other sources (more than $2,000 per capita in 2000). In Massachusetts, around two thirds of tax revenue comes from income taxes. Georgia's fiscal state, by contrast, remains relatively weaker (less than $1,000 per capita in 2000), with only fifty percent of revenue coming from income taxation.

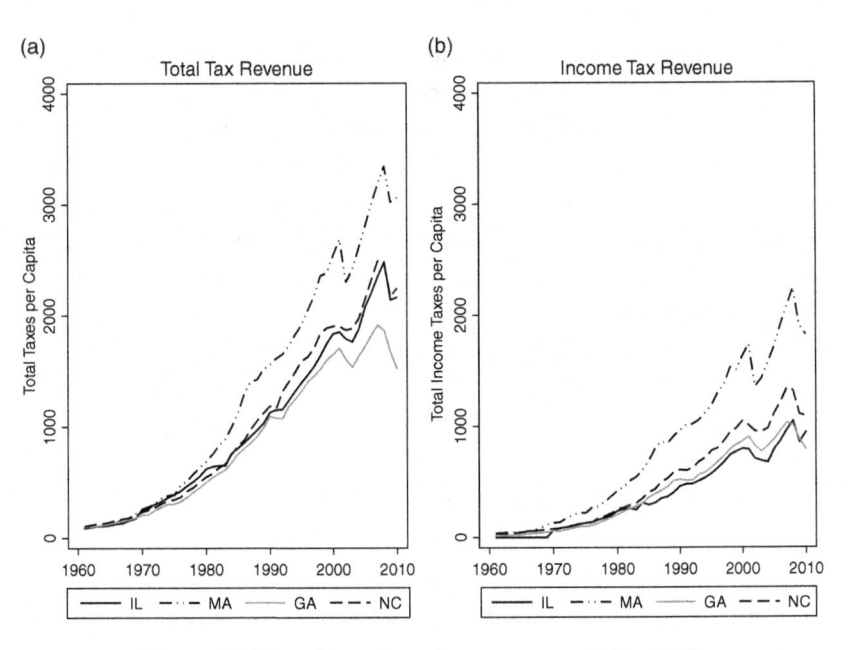

Figure 20 Transformation of states taxes: 1960–2010.

All values per capita. Income taxes include individual and corporate sources. Source: Beramendi et al. (2021).

In between, Illinois and North Carolina are mixed cases: Illinois illustrates a case where the strong industrializing push meets the resistance of entrenched rural interests, whereas North Carolina illustrates better a process of partial industrialization subsidiary to the distribution and export of commodities.

7 How Geography and Industrialization Shape Capacity

In this section we focus on the link between economic geography and industrialization, and investments in fiscal capacity. We argue that uneven economic geography creates political barriers to investments in centralized fiscal capacity and the nature of the industrialization process structures whether political barriers associated with uneven economic geography can be overcome. We focus on the economic incentives behind territorial integration to gain the benefits of early industrialization and the surplus associated with early industrialization as drivers of investments in centralized fiscal capacity. In late industrializers, in contrast, the benefits of industrialization were concentrated primarily in the agricultural sector and thus reinforced the importance of economic geography. Late industrializers also did not experience the surge in growth and revenue, and therefore government surplus, as a result of industrialization. The expansion of public goods, including investments in fiscal capacity, during this transformation is thus far more limited in both scope and space.

In what follows, we provide long-run evidence on how the transformation of the economy during industrialization changes tax collection in early and late industrializing countries. We outline how fiscal capacity investments played out in our focus cases with unequal geographic economic endowments – the USA and Argentina. We then document long-term trends in cross-national data in the collection of all taxes and progressive direct taxes from 1870–2010. Finally, we provide evidence in cross-national regressions of the link between polarized geography, industrialization, and state fiscal capacity. We show that uneven economic endowments and productivity are associated with much lower and less progressive tax collection in late developing nations.

7.1 Geography, Industrialization, and Centralization

The skewed distribution of economic resources and productivity across space creates the potential for conflicts over centralization of resources (Beramendi, 2012; Bolton and Roland, 1997). These conflicts have been shown in advanced industrial democracies to produce lower investments in fiscal capacity and lower expenditures, particularly on policies that span regions (Lee and Rogers, 2019a). We expect those challenges to be much more profound in late industrializers, where spatial inequalities are higher because of uneven development and uneven investments, and where regional cleavages limit agreement on centralized policies (Boone and Simson, 2019).

Our argument emphasizes the economic incentives of industrial elites to seek public goods investments to enhance their productivity. In the majority of major investments, these public goods would be provided by central governments because (1) they provided the infrastructure for international trade (taxed by the central government) and (2) they crossed jurisdictional boundaries. If we consider very large-scale investments such as national railroads or the construction of waterways, moreover, the central government was typically the only level of government with the means to collect large-scale revenue to fund them. The investments associated with economic expansion and development related to industrialization, then, often depended on the power and resources of the central government. Accordingly, the story of central capacity is one of state-building and the rise of national governments.

Soifer (2016) emphasizes how political regionalism, whether based on spatial inequalities or ethnic cleavages, is a direct barrier to centralization and the broad provision of public goods. He provides evidence of these mechanisms in case studies of Ecuador and Colombia, two countries with high spatial inequalities (see Figure 14) and high ethnic diversity, and that saw little public good provision after independence. Elites in the capitals of those nations saw little benefit from providing resources in areas with few economic endowments, did not prefer to redistribute to ethnic out-groups, and generally saw state-building in the area as not worth the investment. Soifer also stresses that ethnicity overlaps with ethnic diversity to limit centralized agreement on public goods provision.

Similarly, our logic hinges on whether economic elites think it is worth the investment in central capacity to provide public goods. In turn, those economic elites expect institutionalized political influence and economic returns in exchange for central taxation (Kao et al., 2019). There is reason to believe that centralized capacity investments are worrisome from the perspective of elites in late developing nations. Gottlieb (2019), for example, argues that elites withhold capacity based on concerns that increased capacity will lead to increased demands for services in the future. Hollenbach and Nascimiento de Silva (2019) show that elites in high-inequality circumstances will withhold fiscal capacity to avoid redistributing to poorer people and places. We expect this to be particularly the case for late industrializers that would have witnessed the expansion of the state in early industrializers, especially the rise of the welfare state in the postwar period. Investments in fiscal capacity are a risky investment that will not be undertaken if the potential benefits exceed the risks. The potential benefits for late industrializers are considerably lower due to the structural features we emphasize – spatial inequalities (perhaps exacerbated by the colonial experience) and lower gains from industrialization. Thus, capacity may be intentionally withheld because of both limited potential returns and potential risks that capacity would be met with higher expectations of government intervention.

7.2 Why Invest in Central Capacity?

Clearly, some nations of the world decided that investments in centralized fiscal capacity were worth the risks involved. In the previous chapters we outlined the fruits of those efforts – broad provision of public goods throughout the space of that nation that reduced spatial inequalities given by nature. In this section we document the evolution of the fiscal state that enabled or impeded those investments.

Evidence from long-term trends in fiscal capacity development help to illuminate the differences across early and late industrializers, and those with low and high dispersion in subnational endowments. In Figure 21 we show how fiscal capacity emerged, as agricultural production fell, from the 1870s to 2010 in the subset of countries studied in Beramendi et al. (2018). We have grouped

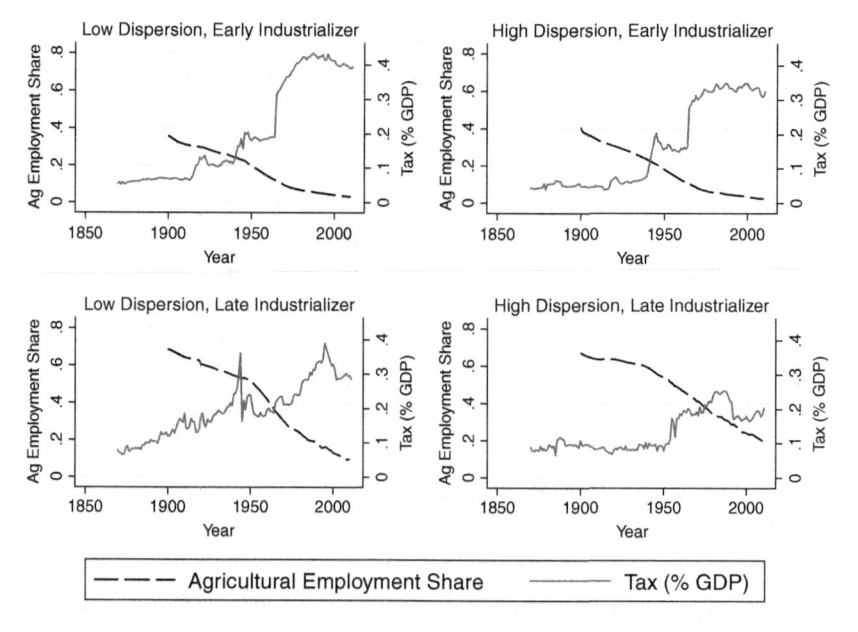

Figure 21 Subnational agricultural endowments, industrialization, and overall fiscal capacity.

Total General Tax Revenue (% GDP) (Beramendi et al., 2018), Agricultural Employment Share (Wingender, 2014).

countries as early or late industrializers using our transition cutoff of 1950 and high or low dispersion as above or below the median dispersion in the sample. We then plot the rise of tax as a percentage of GDP in those nations, along with the fall in the agricultural employment share. The patterns observed are consistent with our account of fiscal development. The low-dispersion early industrializers rise to the highest levels of fiscal capacity (approximately 40 percent of GDP) at the end of the time series (2010). In both the high-dispersion early industrializers (e.g., USA, Canada) and the low-dispersion late industrializers (e.g., Finland, Hungary), the level of fiscal capacity in the sample end at a moderate level, approximately 30 percent of GDP. The lowest level of capacity is found in the high-dispersion late industrializers (e.g., Argentina, Brazil), where tax collection is equivalent to approximately 20 percent of GDP on average. Going from the low-dispersion, early industrializer category to the high-dispersion, late industrializer category represents a fall of approximately 50 percent of revenue as a percentage of GDP.

These investments in fiscal capacity in early industrializers were associated with reforms that were very successful in reducing regional inequalities in countries such as the United States over the twentieth century. Only in the recent decades has regional inequality begun to rise in early industrializers as technological change and economic agglomeration favored growth in the most productive states.

REGIONAL COMPROMISE: THE FEDERAL INCOME TAX IN THE UNITED STATES

The resources that enabled US regional integration came from the federal income tax, enacted via Constitutional amendment in 1913. Passage of a federal income tax was decades in the making and politically fraught. Political conflict over the income tax pitted Northern industrial states along with a few rising Pacific states in opposition against the supportive lower-income Southern and Midwestern states (Baack and Ray, 1985). Three states, Massachusetts, New York, and Pennsylvania, were likely to bear the large majority of the new tax.

Income taxes were a replacement for tariffs, which had long supplied the majority of federal resources. Tariffs initially worked against agricultural producers hoping to sell their products on the international market. Only later would these tariffs also hurt industrial producers who found a comparative advantage relative to Western Europe during World Wars I and II. The income tax thus shifted the cost of the federal government away from the agricultural states onto the industrial and capitalist Northeast (Baack and Ray, 1985). In this sense, the United States acted much like a late developer, with agricultural production boosting support for industrial development via tariffs. The difference for the US federal government in comparison with late developers was the adoption of serious revenue instruments and investments in capacity to collect it. We also see the early versus late industrializing dynamic in state revenue collection, as shown in Section 6.

The passage of the income tax also reflected rising opposition to tariffs in the Northeast. Baack and Ray (1985, p. 620) explain, "Exporters of manufactured goods along with eastern banks and individuals involved in U.S. foreign direct investments were very interested in supporting new methods of funding the federal government that would avoid the deficit problem and permit a reduction in tariffs. The fact that the income-tax amendment was submitted to the states in 1909 and that U.S. tariffs were substantially reduced was neither coincidental nor without historical precedent."

How did the United States manage to put in place a highly effective revenue instrument that imposed high costs on the most productive regions? The answer lies in a spatial log-roll – the three biggest contributors to the income tax would also be its biggest beneficiaries, at least in the short to medium run. The income tax paid for a bolstered US Navy, which secured US trade around the world. The benefits of naval construction were concentrated in New York, Pennsylvania, and Massachusetts. Similarly, the income tax paid the veteran's pension program, providing benefits for Union soldiers concentrated in the Northeast. Thus, supporters of increased naval appropriations and veterans pensions in the Northeast struck a deal with supporters of reduced tariffs and a robust income tax in the South and Midwest.

Figure 22 shows similar patterns for the expansion of progressive taxation as industrialization progresses. For this indicator, all early industrializers, whether high or low dispersion, end up with relatively similar levels of direct tax revenue (income, property, and social security taxation as a percentage of total taxation). In 2010, these sources represent around 75 percent of total taxation in early industrializers. Late industrializers, on the other hand, gain more of their taxation from indirect sources, most notably consumption. Even still, the difference between high- and low-dispersion late industrializers is notable. Low-dispersion late industrializers collect approximately 60 percent of tax revenue from direct sources. In contrast, high-dispersion late industrializers collect around 40 percent of revenue from direct sources. Again, moving from the low-dispersion, early industrializer category of Figure 22 to the high-dispersion, late industrializer category is associated with a drop of around 50 percent of revenue from direct taxes.

Figure 23 summarizes Figures 21 and 22. Emerging from very similar starting points in the late nineteenth century, in which the late industrializers in fact had higher average levels of both total revenue and progressive tax revenue, we see the rise of the early industrializers, especially those with relatively even economic endowments in space. Early industrializers pulled ahead in the early twentieth century and only expanded their lead in the postwar period.

WITHHOLDING REVENUE: TAXATION IN ARGENTINA

Early state-building conflicts in Argentina were focused on the distribution of the revenue from exports that were concentrated in Buenos Aires (Rock, 1987). This center-periphery conflict is critical to understanding the development of the state in Argentina, especially its limited fiscal capacity

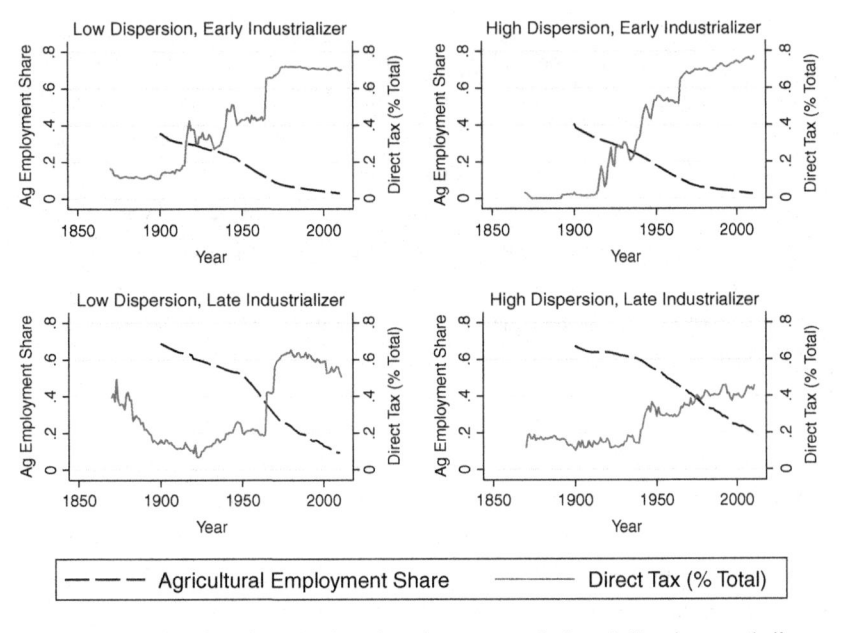

Figure 22 Subnational agricultural endowments, industrialization, and direct taxation.

Total General Tax Revenue (% GDP) (Beramendi et al., 2018), Agricultural Employment Share (Wingender, 2014).

and its focus on interregional redistribution. Debates on the adoption of the income tax in Argentina stressed that the fruits would mainly be culled from the capital city, only to be sent outward to the periphery (Román, 2009). This distributive tension proved crucial, and ultimately the income tax was adopted on a very limited basis, and it has not produced high levels of government revenue (Bergman, 2003; Román, 2012). Current conflicts over revenue distribution in Argentina largely focus on the same issue, in addition to the distribution from the VAT that is collected primarily from the Greater Buenos Aires region.

The fiscal state in Argentina has a heavy emphasis on interregional transfers intended, in theory, to equilibrate strong interregional inequalities (Saiegh and Tommasi, 1999). Revenue sharing between the federal government and the provinces is the central fiscal issue in Argentina and is politically fraught (Eaton, 2001; Gibson et al., 2004). The worry for the richest provinces in these arrangements is that their resources will be redistributed outward. For this reason, the richest provinces have sought to

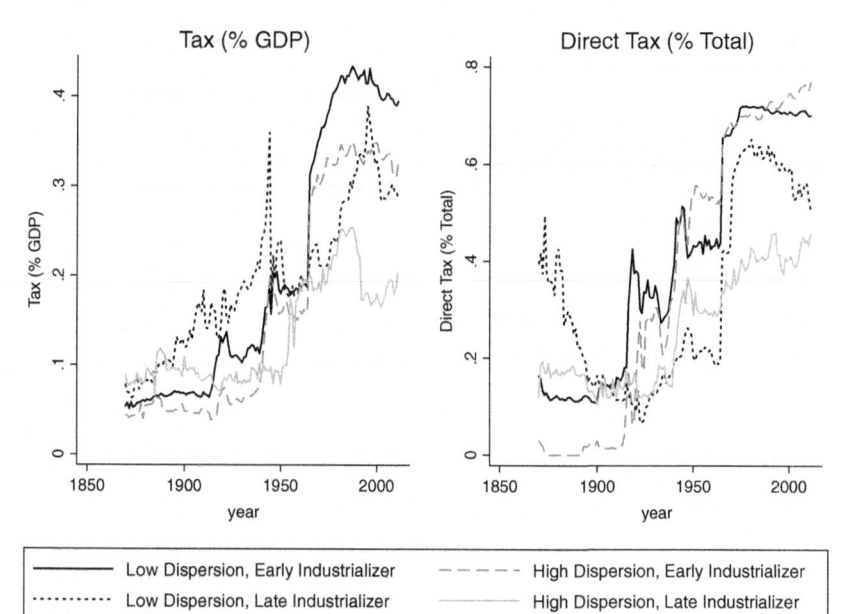

Figure 23 Subnational agricultural endowments, industrialization, and fiscal capacity.

Total General Tax Revenue (% GDP) (Beramendi et al., 2018), Agricultural Employment Share (Wingender, 2014).

withhold resources from the central pot, with a preference to keep resources within their subnational borders (Díaz-Cayeros, 2006). These tensions highlight the centralization problem in Argentina that keeps national tax resources low.

Argentina notoriously underperforms in the extraction of fiscal revenue, including relative to its neighbors at similar levels of development (Bergman, 2003). Despite its relative income, it collects a low amount of revenue and relies heavily on regressive taxation – especially tariffs, export taxation, and the VAT.

The consequences of underinvestments in fiscal capacity are profound. Low state capacity has been associated with less economic development (Besley and Persson, 2013), more civil conflict (Fearon and Laitin, 2003), more economic crises (Boone, 1990; Fukuyama, 2004), and higher inequality (Soifer, 2013). For our purposes we see these underinvestments in fiscal capacity as the root cause of dramatic divergence in the politics of inequality and redistribution

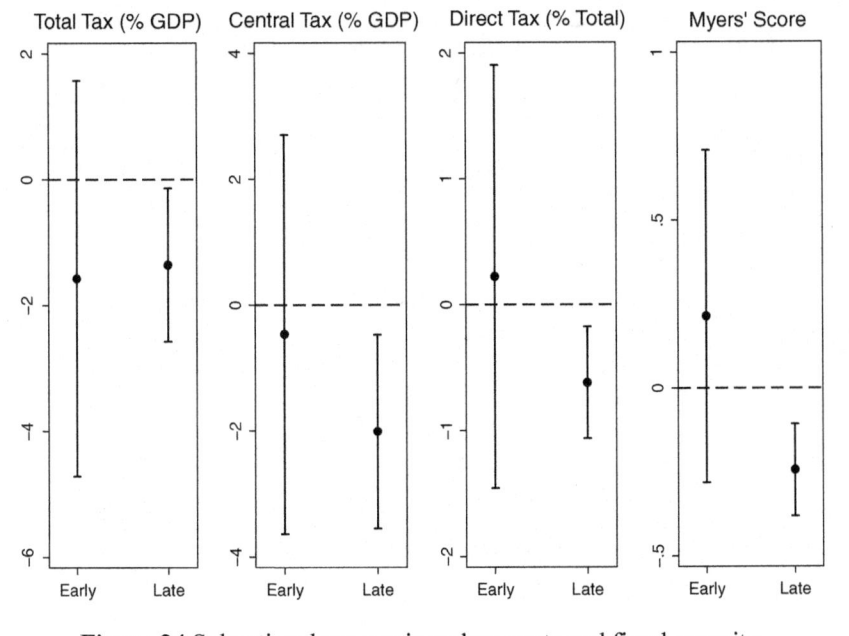

Figure 24 Subnational economic endowments and fiscal capacity.

Cross-sectional data of national mean values. Independent variable: Coefficient of variation in subnational economic endowments. Dependent variables: Total General Tax Revenue (% GDP) (Prichard, 2016), Total Central Tax Revenue (% GDP), Direct Taxes (% Total Tax Revenue) (Beramendi et al., 2018), Census Myers' Score (Lee and Zhang, 2017).

across advanced industrial societies and less developed nations, as we discuss in Volume II.

7.3 Regression Analysis: Geography, Industrialization, and Capacity

In this section we examine the empirical link between uneven economic geography and fiscal capacity, conditional on the timing on industrialization, for our full sample of nations. In Figure 24 we show results across four different dependent variables to capture fiscal capacity – general tax collection (% GDP), central tax collection (% GDP), direct tax collection (% total taxes), and state "legibility," measured with the Myers' Score (D'Arcy and Nistotskaya, 2017; Lee and Zhang, 2017).[21] In each chart the coefficients for early and late industrializers, and their standard errors, are shown. Across the four dependent variables, we see that subnational variation in economic endowments is not a strong predictor of fiscal capacity in early industrializers. While the coefficient

---

[21] Full results in Appendix 2.2.

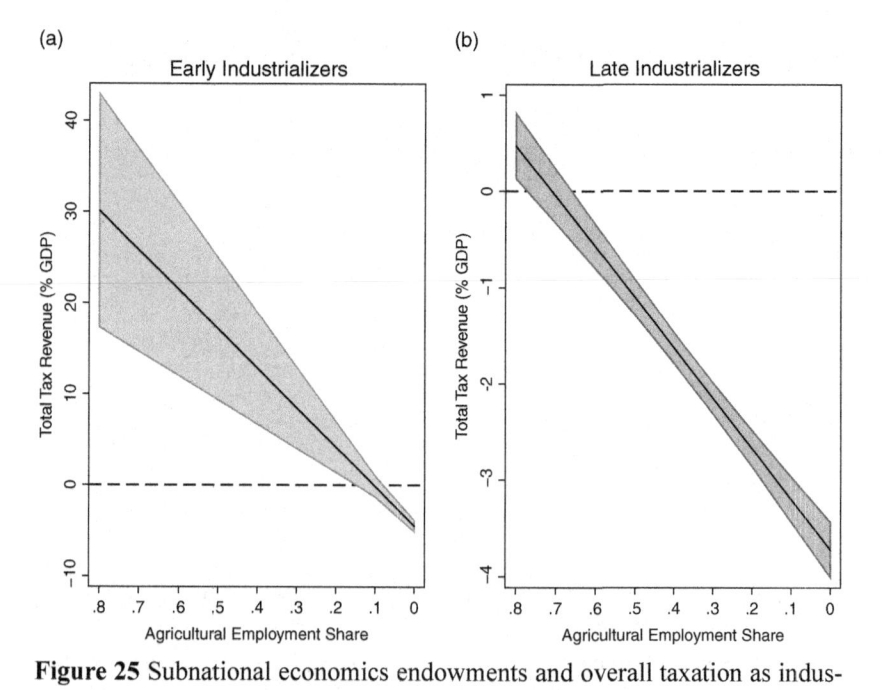

Figure 25 Subnational economics endowments and overall taxation as industrialization progresses.

Total Tax Revenue (% GDP) (Prichard et al., 2014), Agricultural Employment Share (Wingender, 2014).

is negative across the three tax indicators, the results do not approach statistical significance. In the case of direct taxation and the Myers' score, uneven economic geography is even associated with positive state capacity on average, although the results are not significant.

The results for late industrializers in Figure 24, however, show that uneven economic geography is a strong predictor of low fiscal capacity in these nations. In the four indicators we see that the subnational variation in economic endowments is strongly and significantly associated with lower fiscal capacity. This result is an important precondition for our theory, namely that uneven geography may have hindered fiscal capacity development more in late industrializers. Across the full sample of countries, uneven economic geography is a very strong predictor of weak fiscal capacity, but this result is primarily driven by the late industrial and preindustrial nations.

Figure 25 provides an additional examination of the temporal dynamics of fiscal capacity development in early and late industrializers. Figure 25(a) plots the conditional effect of variation in subnational economic endowments on total tax collection (% GDP) as agricultural employment falls (our measure

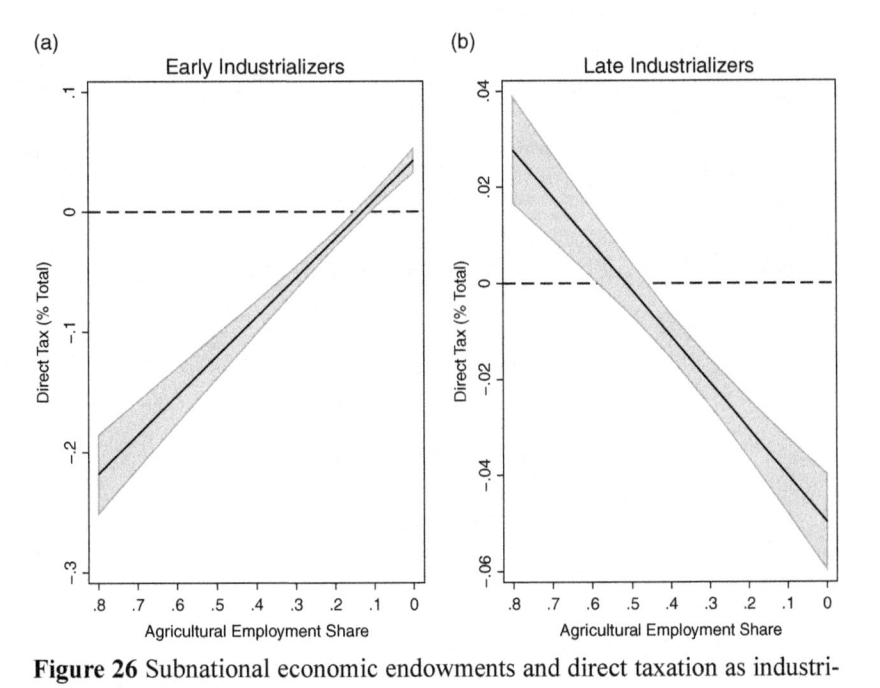

Figure 26 Subnational economic endowments and direct taxation as industrialization progresses, 1870–2010.

Direct Tax Revenue (% Total Tax Revenue) (Beramendi et al., 2018), Agricultural Employment Share (Wingender, 2014).

of industrial growth). The black lines in Figure 25 show the predicted effect of subnational variation in economic endowments, at its mean value, across different stages of industrial development. In early industrializers, the countries with diverse endowments in fact collected higher levels of taxes at the beginning stages of industrialization. It was only at the final stages of industrialization that they began to collect significantly lower levels of tax revenue. For late industrializers, on the other hand, uneven economic endowments appear to be a liability at every phase of industrialization, as shown in Figure 25(b). For late industrializers, high variation in subnational economic geography drags down tax collection as the country becomes increasingly industrialized, holding all other factors equal.

Figure 26 shows how the different patterns emerge for direct taxation on income and property across early and late industrializers in the period 1870–2010. In early industrializers, shown in Figure 26(a), the predicted effect of variation in subnational economic endowments is negative early on in the industrialization process. It is only as industrialization becomes fully entrenched (agricultural employment falls to 25 percent of employment or less) that we see a uneven economic geography become a neutral or positive contributor to direct tax collection. At the highest levels of industrialization, variation in economic endowments is associated with significantly higher direct taxation. This likely reflects the particular emphasis on direct taxation in high-dispersion anglophone federations like the USA, Canada, and Australia. In Figure 26(b), showing the late industrializing nations, we do not see the predicted effect of uneven economic geography as a neutral or positive contributor to direct taxation. At low levels of industrialization, direct taxation is slightly higher in places with uneven geography, perhaps reflecting relative ease in collecting revenue from concentrated agriculture production. As industrialization increases, however, we see that direct taxation falls in late industrializers. Once a nation passes the "industrialized" threshold of less than 50 percent agricultural employment, high variation in subnational economic geography is associated with significantly lower direct taxation in late industrializers.

Our analysis shows a consistent negative effect of high variation in subnational economic geography on fiscal capacity in late industrializing nations. This drives a critical wedge between advanced industrial societies and late industrializers. For the former, fiscal capacity is assumed. For the latter, the more limited capacity changes politics altogether. Soifer (2013) has shown just how crucial fiscal capacity is in the context of distributive conflicts. While elites may fear democracy due to concerns with redistribution (Acemoglu and Robinson, 2006a; Boix, 2003), they are less likely to resist democratization when fiscal capacity is low. Soifer argues, "state capacity is necessary for redistribution, and where extractive capacity is lacking, rational economic elites should not fear that suffrage expansion would lead to effective redistribution, nor should the masses expect to gain economically from democratization. State capacity thus acts as a scope condition for the effect of inequality on regime outcomes" (p. 1). The reason behind this contrast is that state fiscal capacity conditions the politics of redistribution, both to people and to places.

8 Conclusion: from Capacity to Redistribution

In this volume, we have shown how the politics of capacity development is spatial. We have provided systematic evidence about the connection between different industrialization processes and the politics of capacity development. Early industrializers tend to integrate space internally and conquer space externally. Late industrializers are far more constrained in their options and show more skewed patterns of geographic concentration of economic and political power. We have shown how these differences shape the early stages in the process of capacity building. We have also shown how these initial differences help make sense of heterogeneous development of capacity in response to structural economic changes and international conflict. In the next volume we develop the final piece in our story – how economic geography and the timing of industrialization are linked to long-run differences in redistribution and inequality. We develop three themes.

First, what governs the persistence over the long run of the low capacity–high spatial inequality equilibrium described in this volume? Our analysis places particular emphasis on the role played in this process by two political institutions: legislative malapportionment and decentralized federalism.

Second, how does capacity condition the nature of redistribution? In our view, it does so by fostering three fundamental characteristics. Redistributive systems are smaller, persistently inefficient, and perverse when capacity is low. They are smaller because, rather intuitively, a direct consequence of low capacity and high geographical skew is a reduction in the amount of redistribution effectively provided by the state (something that, as we will show, also happens at the margin among early industrializers). They are persistently inefficient because the very nature of distributive politics in these places prevents them from undertaking capacity investments even when revenue inflows lift the resource constraint. We argue that skewed patterns of economic and political power contribute significantly to this type of distributive politics. And they are perverse because by and large these are systems that are relatively regressive, and the regressive nature of redistribution is a major factor undermining both democratic accountability and economic equality.

Third, the capacity-redistribution link, and its historical origins, helps illuminate important unexplained aspects of the evolution of inequality in the world today. They also have significant implications for important questions about the workings of democracy today. We close Volume II with a succinct discussion of these issues and a systematic discussion of the ways political regimes can overcome capacity gaps.

References

Acemoglu, D. and Johnson, S. (2005). Unbundling institutions. *Journal of Political Economy*, 113(5):949–995.

Acemoglu, D., Johnson, S., and Robinson, J. A. (2001). The colonial origins of comparative development: an empirical investigation. *American Economic Review*, 91(5):1369–1401.

Acemoglu, D. and Robinson, J. (2006a). *Economic origins of dictatorship and democracy*. Cambridge University Press.

Acemoglu, D. and Robinson, J. A. (2006b). Economic backwardness in political perspective. *American Political Science Review*, 100(1):115–131.

Acemoglu, D. and Robinson, J. A. (2019). *The narrow corridor: states, societies, and the fate of liberty*. Penguin.

Acemoglu, D. and Wolitzky, A. (2011). The economics of labor coercion. *Econometrica*, 79(2):555–600.

Adebusoye, P. M. et al. (2006). Geographic labour mobility in sub-Saharan Africa. *International Development Research Centre (IDRC) Working Paper*, 1. International Development Research Centre.

Aidt, T. S. and Jensen, P. S. (2009). The taxman tools up: an event history study of the introduction of the personal income tax. *Journal of Public Economics*, 93(1):160–175.

Aidt, T. S. and Jensen, P. S. (2014). Workers of the world, unite! Franchise extensions and the threat of revolution in Europe, 1820–1938. *European Economic Review*, 72:52–75.

Alapuro, R. (1981). Origins of agrarian socialism in Finland. In: Torsvik, P. (ed.), *Mobilization. Center-Periphery. Structures and Nation-Building. A Volume in Commemoration of Stein Rokkan, Universitetsforlaget, Oslo, Norway*, pages 274–295.

Albertus, M. (2015). *Autocracy and redistribution*. Cambridge University Press.

Albertus, M. and Menaldo, V. (2014). Gaming democracy: elite dominance during transition and the prospects for redistribution. *British Journal of Political Science*, 44(3):575–603.

Alestalo, M. and Kuhnle, S. (1986). The Scandinavian route: economic, social, and political developments in Denmark, Finland, Norway, and Sweden. *International Journal of Sociology*, 16(3–4):1–38.

Allen, R. C. (2009). *The British industrial revolution in global perspective*. Cambridge University Press.

Allen, R. C., Murphy, T. E., and Schneider, E. B. (2012). The colonial origins of the divergence in the Americas: a labor market approach. *The Journal of Economic History*, 72(4):863–894.

Alston, L. J. and Ferrie, J. P. (1999). *Southern paternalism and the American welfare state: economics, politics, and institutions in the South, 1865–1965*. Cambridge University Press.

Amat, F. and Beramendi, P. (2020). Democracy under high inequality: capacity, spending, and participation. *The Journal of Politics*, 82(3):859–878.

Ansell, B. W. and Samuels, D. J. (2014). *Inequality and democratization: an elite-competition approach*. Cambridge University Press.

Ardanaz, M. and Scartascini, C. (2013). Inequality and personal income taxation: the origins and effects of legislative malapportionment. *Comparative Political Studies*, 46(12):1636–1663.

Baack, B. D. and Ray, E. J. (1985). Special interests and the adoption of the income tax in the United States. *The Journal of Economic History*, 45(3):607–625.

Baer, W. (1972). Import substitution and industrialization in Latin America: experiences and interpretations. *Latin American Research Review*, 7(1):95 122.

Barro, R. J. (1988). Government spending in a simple model of endogenous growth. 2nd ed. Technical report.

Barro, R. J. and Sala-i Martin, X. (1992). Convergence. *Journal of Political Economy*, 100(2):223–251.

Bates, R. H. (2005). *Markets and states in tropical Africa: the political basis of agricultural policies*. 1st ed. University of California Press.

Bates, R. H. (2014). *Markets and states in tropical Africa: the political basis of agricultural policies*. 2nd ed. University of California Press.

Bensel, R. F. et al. (2000). *The political economy of American industrialization, 1877–1900*. Cambridge University Press.

Bentzen, J. S., Kaarsen, N., and Wingender, A. M. (2013). The timing of industrialization across countries. Technical report, University of Copenhagen.

Beramendi, P. (2012). *The political geography of inequality: regions and redistribution*. Cambridge University Press.

Beramendi, P., Cassidy, T., Dincecco, M., and Rogers, M. (2021). Fiscal development in the US states. *Duke University Working Paper*.

Beramendi, P., Dincecco, M., and Rogers, M. (2018). Intra-elite competition and long-run fiscal development. *Journal of Politics*, 81(1), 49–65.

Beramendi, P. and Queralt, D. (2014). The electoral origins of the fiscal state. Technical report, Duke University.

Bergman, M. S. (2003). Tax reforms and tax compliance: the divergent paths of Chile and Argentina. *Journal of Latin American Studies*, 35(3):593–624.

Berkowitz, D. and Clay, K. B. (2011). *The evolution of a nation: how geography and law shaped the American states*. Princeton University Press.

Besley, T. and Persson, T. (2009). The origins of state capacity: property rights, taxation, and politics. *The American Economic Review*, 99(4):1218–1244.

Besley, T. and Persson, T. (2011). *Pillars of prosperity: the political economics of development clusters*. Princeton University Press.

Besley, T. and Persson, T. (2013). Taxation and development. *Handbook of Public Economics*, 5:51–107.

Bigsten, A. (2016). Determinants of the evolution of inequality in Africa. *Journal of African Economies*, 27(1):127–148.

Bogart, D. (2005). Turnpike trusts and the transportation revolution in 18th century England. *Explorations in Economic History*, 42(4):479–508.

Boix, C. (2003). *Democracy and redistribution*. Cambridge University Press.

Boix, C. (2015). *Political order and inequality*. Cambridge University Press.

Boix, C. (2019). *Democratic capitalism at the crossroads: technological change and the future of politics*. Princeton University Press.

Bolton, P. and Roland, G. (1997). The breakup of nations: a political economy analysis. *The Quarterly Journal of Economics*, 112(4), pages 1057–1090.

Boone, C. (1990). State power and economic crisis in Senegal. *Comparative Politics*, 22(3):341–357.

Boone, C. (2003). *Political topographies of the African state: territorial authority and institutional choice*. Cambridge University Press.

Boone, C. (2012). Territorial politics and the reach of the state: unevenness by design. *Revista de ciencia política*, 32(3):623–641.

Boone, C. and Simson, R. (2019). Regional inequalities in African political economy: theory, conceptualization and measurement, and political effects. Working paper, London School of Economics.

Boone, C. and Wahman, M. (2015). Rural bias in African electoral systems: legacies of unequal representation in African democracies. *Electoral Studies*, 40:335–346.

Brambor, T., Lindvall, J., and Stjernquist, A. (2013). Ideology of heads of government, 1870–2012 (version 1.2). Technical report, Department of Political Science, Lund University.

Cai, H. and Treisman, D. (2005). Does competition for capital discipline governments? Decentralization, globalization, and public policy. *American Economic Review*, 95(3):817–830.

Cardoso, F. H. and Faletto, E. (1979). *Dependency and development in Latin America (Dependencia y desarrollo en América Latina, engl.).* University of California Press.

Carlson, C. (2019). Agrarian structure and underdevelopment in Latin America: Bringing the latifundio "back in". *Latin American Research Review*, 54(3), 678–693.

Carrascal-Incera, A., McCann, P., Ortega-Argilés, R., and Rodríguez-Pose, A. (2020). UK interregional inequality in a historical and international comparative context. *National Institute Economic Review*, 253:R4–R17.

Castles, F. G. (1973). Barrington Moore's thesis and Swedish political development. *Government and Opposition*, 8(3):313–331.

Centeno, M. A. (2002). *Blood and debt: war and the nation-state in Latin America.* Pennsylvania State University Press.

Choe, S.-C., Lee, K. S., and Pahk, K.-H. (1987). Determinants of locational choice of manufacturing firms in the Seoul region: an analysis of survey results. World Bank Discussion Paper. Report No. UDD-85.

Chun, D. H. and Lee, K. S. (1985). Changing location patterns of population and employment in the Seoul region. Number UDD-65. World Bank.

Cipolla, C. M. (2013). *The economic decline of empires.* Routledge.

Collier, R. B. and Collier, D. (2002). *Shaping the political arena.* University of Notre Dame Press.

Congleton, R. D. (2010). *Perfecting parliament: constitutional reform, liberalism, and the rise of western democracy.* Cambridge University Press.

Cox, G. W. (2016). *Marketing sovereign promises: monopoly brokerage and the growth of the English state.* Cambridge University Press.

D'Arcy, M. and Nistotskaya, M. (2017). State first, then democracy: using cadastral records to explain governmental performance in public goods provision. *Governance*, 30(2):193–209.

Dasgupta, A. (2020). Explaining rural conservatism: technological and political change in the Great Plains. Working paper, University of California Merced.

Dell, M. (2010). The persistent effects of Peru's mining mita. *Econometrica*, 78(6):1863–1903.

Dell, M., Jones, B. F., and Olken, B. A. (2012). Temperature shocks and economic growth: evidence from the last half century. *American Economic Journal: Macroeconomics*, 4(3):66–95.

Demographia (2019). Demographia world urban areas. Accessed at www.demographia.com/db-worldua.pdf

Diamond, J. (2013). *Guns, germs and steel: a short history of everybody for the last 13,000 years.* Random House.

Díaz-Cayeros, A. (2006). *Federalism, fiscal authority, and centralization in Latin America.* Cambridge University Press.

Diaz-Cayeros, A., Estévez, F., and Magaloni, B. (2016). *The political logic of poverty relief: electoral strategies and social policy in Mexico.* Cambridge University Press.

Dincecco, M. (2011). *Political Transformations and Public Finances: Europe, 1650–1913.* Cambridge University Press.

Dincecco, M. (2017). *State capacity and economic development: present and past.* Cambridge University Press.

Dincecco, M. and Onorato, M. G. (2018). *From warfare to wealth.* Cambridge University Press.

Easterly, W. (2007). Inequality does cause underdevelopment: insights from a new instrument. *Journal of Development Economics*, 84(2):755–776.

Eaton, K. (2001). Decentralisation, democratisation and liberalisation: the history of revenue sharing in Argentina, 1934–1999. *Journal of Latin American Studies*, 33(1):1–28.

Edwards, S. (1993). Openness, trade liberalization, and growth in developing countries. *Journal of Economic Literature*, 31(3):1358–1393.

Engerman, S. L. and Sokoloff, K. L. (1997). Factor endowments, institutions, and differential paths of growth among new world economies. In Stephen Haber (ed.), *How Latin America fell behind*, pages 260–304. Stanford University Press.

Engerman, S. L. and Sokoloff, K. L. (2002). Factor endowments, inequality, and paths of development among new world economics. Working Paper 9259. National Bureau of Economic Research. www.nber.org/papers/w9259

Evans, P. B. (2012). *Embedded autonomy: states and industrial transformation.* Princeton University Press.

FAO (2012). Global Agro-Ecological Zones (GAEZ v3.0). *IIASA, Laxenburg, Austria and FAO, Rome, Italy.* FAO & IIASA.

Fearon, J. D. and Laitin, D. D. (2003). Ethnicity, insurgency, and civil war. *American Political Science Review*, 97(1):75–90.

Fremdling, R. (1977). Railroads and German economic growth: a leading sector analysis with a comparison to the United States and Great Britain. *The Journal of Economic History*, 37(3):583–604.

Fukuyama, F. (2004). The imperative of state-building. *Journal of Democracy*, 15(2):17–31.

Galor, O., Moav, O., and Vollrath, D. (2009). Inequality in landownership, the emergence of human-capital promoting institutions, and the great divergence. *The Review of Economic Studies*, 76(1):143–179.

Gans-Morse, J., Mazzuca, S., and Nichter, S. (2014). Varieties of clientelism: machine politics during elections. *American Journal of Political Science*, 58(2):415–432.

Garfias, F. et al. (2018). Elite competition and state capacity development: theory and evidence from post-revolutionary Mexico. *American Political Science Review*, 112(2):339–357.

Gerschenkron, A. (1962). Economic backwardness in historical perspective (1962). *The Political Economy Reader: Markets as Institutions*, pages 211–228.

Gerschenkron, A. (1962). *Economic backwardness in historical perspective*. Belknap, Cambridge, MA.

Gibson, E., Calvo, E., and Falleti, T. (2004). Reallocative federalism: legislative overrepresentation and public spending in the Western hemisphere. In Edward Gibson (ed.), *Federalism and democracy in Latin America*, pages 173–196. Johns Hopkins University Press.

Glaeser, E. (2011). *Triumph of the city*. Pan.

Gottlieb, J. (2019). Keeping the state weak to prevent collective claim-making in young democracies.

Grossman, G. and Lewis, J. I. (2014). Administrative unit proliferation. *American Political Science Review*, pages 196–217.

Haber, S. (2005). Development strategy or endogenous process? The industrialization of Latin America. Technical report, Stanford University.

Haggard, S. (1990). *Pathways from the periphery: the politics of growth in the newly industrializing countries*. Cornell University Press.

Haggard, S. (2018). *Developmental states*. Cambridge University Press.

Hanson, J. K. (2014). Forging then taming Leviathan: state capacity, constraints on rulers, and development. *International Studies Quarterly*, 58(2):380–392.

Hanson, J. K. (2015). Democracy and state capacity: complements or substitutes? *Studies in Comparative International Development*, 50(3):304–330.

Hauner, T., Milanovic, B., and Naidu, S. (2017). Inequality, foreign investment, and imperialism. *Stone Center Working Paper*, 2017. Accessed at https://ssrn.com/abstract=3089701.

Henderson, J. V., Squires, T., Storeygard, A., and Weil, D. (2017). The global distribution of economic activity: nature, history, and the role of trade. *The Quarterly Journal of Economics*, 133(1):357–406.

Henderson, V. (2002). Urbanization in developing countries. *The World Bank Research Observer*, 17(1):89–112.

Herbst, J. (2014). *States and power in Africa: comparative lessons in authority and control*. Princeton University Press.

Hobsbawm, E. (1989). *The age of empire: 1875–1914*. Vintage.

Hobsbawm, E. J. (1968). *Industry and empire: an economic history of Britain since 1750*. Weidenfeld and Nicolson.

Hollenbach, F. M. (2019). Elite interests and public spending: evidence from Prussian cities. *The Review of International Organizations*, 16: 189–211.

Hollenbach, F. M. and Nascimiento de Silva, T. (2019). Fiscal capacity and inequality: evidence from Brazilian municipalities. *The Journal of Politics*, 81(4):1434–1445.

Hora, R. (2002). Landowning bourgeoisie or business bourgeoisie? On the peculiarities of the Argentine economic elite, 1880–1945. *Journal of Latin American Studies*, 34(3):587–623.

Huillery, E. (2009). History matters: the long-term impact of colonial public investments in French West Africa. *American Economic Journal: Applied Economics*, 1(2):176–215.

Hunt, E. H. (1986). Industrialization and regional inequality: wages in Britain, 1760–1914. *The Journal of Economic History*, 46(4):935–966.

Ichino, N. and Nathan, N. L. (2013). Do primaries improve electoral performance? Clientelism and intra-party conflict in Ghana. *American Journal of Political Science*, 57(2):428–441.

Isciences (2008). Elevation and depth v2 2000 (dataset).

Iversen, T. and Soskice, D. (2019). *Democracy and prosperity: reinventing capitalism through a turbulent century*. Princeton University Press.

Jaworski, T. (2017). World War II and the industrialization of the American South. *The Journal of Economic History*, 77(4):1048–1082.

Jedwab, R. and Moradi, A. (2016). The permanent effects of transportation revolutions in poor countries: evidence from Africa. *Review of Economics and Statistics*, 98(2):268–284.

Jian, T., Sachs, J. D., and Warner, A. M. (1996). Trends in regional inequality in China. *China Economic Review*, 7(1):1–21.

Joll, J. and Martel, G. (2013). *The origins of the First World War*. Routledge.

Justman, M. and Gradstein, M. (1999). The Industrial Revolution, political transition, and the subsequent decline in inequality in 19th-century Britain. *Explorations in Economic History*, 36(2):109–127.

Kaldor, N. (1963). Taxation for economic development. *The Journal of Modern African Studies*, 1(1):7–23.

Kanbur, R. and Zhang, X. (2005). Fifty years of regional inequality in China: a journey through central planning, reform, and openness. *Review of Development Economics*, 9(1):87–106.

Kao, J., Lu, X., and Queralt, D. (2019). Expected return for taxation: do elites differ from nonelites? University of Texas Working Paper.

Kasara, K. and Suryanarayan, P. (2020). Bureaucratic capacity and class voting: evidence from across the world and the United States. *The Journal of Politics*, 82(3):1097–1112.

Keeling, D. J. (1993). Transport and regional development in Argentina: structural deficiencies and patterns of network evolution. In *Yearbook. Conference of Latin Americanist Geographers*, pages 25–34. JSTOR.

Kitschelt, H. (2000). Linkages between citizens and politicians in democratic polities. *Comparative Political Studies*, 33(6–7):845–879.

Kohli, A. (2004). *State-directed development: political power and industrialization in the global periphery*. Cambridge University Press.

Kohli, A. (2019). *Imperialism and the developing world: how Britain and the United States shaped the global periphery*. Oxford University Press.

Kornai, J. (1992). *The socialist system: the political economy of communism*. Oxford University Press.

Korpi, W. (2006). Power resources and employer-centered approaches in explanations of welfare states and varieties of capitalism: protagonists, consenters, and antagonists. *World Politics*, 58(2):167–206.

Krugman, P. and Elizondo, R. L. (1996). Trade policy and the Third World metropolis. *Journal of Development Economics*, 49(1):137–150.

Krugman, P. and Venables, A. J. (1995). Globalization and the inequality of nations. *The Quarterly Journal of Economics*, 110(4):857–880.

Krugman, P. R. (1991). *Geography and trade*. Massachusetts Institute of Technology Press.

Kuhnle, S. (2013). The Scandinavian path to welfare. In *Resisting punitiveness in Europe?*, pages 90–102. Routledge.

Kurtz, M. J. (2013). *Latin American state building in comparative perspective: social foundations of institutional order*. Cambridge University Press.

Kuznets, P. W. (1988). An East Asian model of economic development: Japan, Taiwan, and South Korea. *Economic Development and Cultural Change*, 36(S3):S11–S43.

Kuznets, S. (1955). Economic growth and income inequality. *The American Economic Review*, 45(1):1–28.

Lee, A. (2019). *Development in multiple dimensions: social power and regional policy in India*. University of Michigan Press.

Lee, D.-w. and Rogers, M. (2019a). Inter-regional inequality and the dynamics of government spending. *Journal of Politics*, 81(2): 487–504.

Lee, D.-w. and Rogers, M. (2019b). Measuring geographic distribution for political research. *Political Analysis*, 27(3): 263–280.

Lee, M. M. and Zhang, N. (2017). Legibility and the informational foundations of state capacity. *The Journal of Politics*, 79(1):118–132.

Lenin, V. I. (1999). *Imperialism: the highest stage of capitalism*. Resistance Books.

Lessmann, C. (2012). Regional inequality and decentralization: an empirical analysis. *Environment and Planning A*, 44(6):1363–1388.

Lindert, P. H. (2004). *Growing public: volume 1, social spending and economic growth since the eighteenth century*, volume 1. Cambridge University Press.

Lizzeri, A. and Persico, N. (2004). Why did the elites extend the suffrage? Democracy and the scope of government, with an application to Britain's age of reform. *The Quarterly Journal of Economics*, 119: 707–765.

Magaloni, B., Diaz-Cayeros, A., and Estévez, F. (2007). Clientelism and portfolio diversification: a model of electoral investment with applications to Mexico. *Patrons, clients, and policies: patterns of democratic accountability and political competition*, pages 182–205.

Mann, M. (1984). The autonomous power of the state: its origins, mechanisms and results. *European Journal of Sociology*, 25(2):185–213.

Mares, I. and Queralt, D. (2015). The non-democratic origins of income taxation. *Comparative Political Studies*, 48(14):1974–2009.

Mazucca, S. L. (2017). Critical juncture and legacies: state formation and economic performance in Latin America. *Qualitative and Multi-Method Research*, 15(1):29–35.

Mitchell, T. D. and Jones, P. D. (2005). An improved method of constructing a database of monthly climate observations and associated high-resolution grids. *International Journal of Climatology*, 25(6):693–712.

Moon, D. (2014). *The Russian peasantry 1600–1930: the world the peasants made*. Routledge.

Moore, B. et al. (1993). *Social origins of dictatorship and democracy: lord and peasant in the making of the modern world*, volume 268. Beacon Press.

Morris, C. T. and Adelman, I. (1980). The religious factor in economic development. *World Development*, 8(7–8):491–501.

Nugent, J. B. and Robinson, J. A. (2010). Are factor endowments fate? *Revista de Historia Economica — Journal of Iberian and Latin American Economic History* 28(1). DOI: https://doi.org/10.1017/S0212610909990048

Nunn, N. (2008). *Slavery, inequality, and economic development in the Americas: an examination of the Engerman-Sokoloff Hypothesis*, pages 148–180. Harvard University Press, Cambridge.

O'Rourke, K. H., de la Escosura, L. P., and Daudin, G. (2010). Trade and empire. In Broadberry, S. and O'Rourke, K. H. (eds.), *The Cambridge Economic History of Modern Europe*, volume 2, pages 96–120.

Østerud, Ø. (1978). *Agrarian structure and peasant politics in Scandinavia. A comparative study of rural response to economic change*. Universitetsforlaget.

Pan, S.-h., Ban, S. H., Mun, P.-l., and Perkins, D. H. (1980). *Rural development*, volume 89. Harvard University Asia Center.

Paniagua, V. (2018). *Protecting Capital: Economic Elites, Asset Portfolio Diversification, and the Politics of Distribution*. PhD thesis, Duke University.

Pierskalla, J., Schultz, A., Wibbels, E., et al. (2017). Order, distance, and local development over the long-run. *Quarterly Journal of Political Science*, 12(4):375–404.

Piketty, T. (2014). *Capital in the twenty-first century*. Belknap Press.

Pincus, S. C. and Robinson, J. A. (2014). What really happened during the Glorious Revolution? In *Institutions, property rights, and economic growth: the legacy of Douglass North*, page 192. Cambridge University Press.

Prichard, W. (2016). Reassessing tax and development research: a new dataset, new findings, and lessons for research. *World Development*, 80:48–60.

Prichard, W., Cobham, A., and Goodall, A. (2014). The ICTD government revenue dataset.

Puga, D. (1998). Urbanization patterns: European versus less developed countries. *Journal of Regional Science*, 38(2):231–252.

Puga, D. and Venables, A. J. (1996). The spread of industry: spatial agglomeration in economic development. *Journal of the Japanese and International Economies*, 10(4):440–464.

Queralt, D. (2015). From mercantilism to free trade: a history of fiscal capacity building. *Quarterly Journal of Political Science*, 10(2): 221–273.

Queralt, D. (2019). War, international finance, and fiscal capacity in the long run. *International Organization*, 73(4):713–753.

Ramankutty, N., Foley, J. A., Norman, J., and McSweeney, K. (2002). The global distribution of cultivable lands: current patterns and sensitivity to possible climate change. *Global Ecology and Biogeography*, 11(5):377–392.

Rock, D. (1987). *Argentina, 1516–1987: From Spanish colonization to Alphonsín. (Updated)*. University of California Press.

Roessler, P., Pengl, Y. I., Marty, R. et al. (2020). The cash crop revolution, colonialism and legacies of spatial inequality: evidence from Africa. CSAE Working Paper Series, 2020–12. Centre for the Study of African Economies, University of Oxford.

Rogers, M. (2016). Inequality and democratic representation in Latin America. In Foweraker, J. and Treviso, D. (eds.), *Democracy and its discontents in Latin America*. Lynne Reinner Press.

Rogers, M. Z. (2015). *The politics of place and the limits to redistribution.* Routledge Press.

Rogers, M. Z. and Weller, N. (2014). Income taxation and the validity of state capacity indicators. *Journal of Public Policy*, 34(2):183–206.

Román, J. A. S. (2009). Economic elites, regional cleavages, and the first attempts at introducing the income tax in Argentina. *Hispanic American Historical Review*, 89(2):253–283.

Román, J. A. S. (2012). *Taxation and society in twentieth-century Argentina.* Springer.

Rostow, W. W. (1959). The stages of economic growth. *The Economic History Review*, 12(1):1–16.

Sachs, J. D. (2001). Tropical underdevelopment. Working Paper 8119. National Bureau of Economic Research. DOI: https://doi.org/10.3386/w8119

Sachs, J. D. (2003). Institutions don't rule: direct effects of geography on per capita income. Working Paper 9490. National Bureau of Economic Research. DOI: https://doi.org/10.3386/w9490

Saiegh, S. M. and Tommasi, M. (1999). Why is Argentina's fiscal federalism so inefficient? Entering the labyrinth. *Journal of Applied Economics*, 2(1):169–209.

Sala-i Martin, X. X. (1996). The classical approach to convergence analysis. *The Economic Journal*, 106(437): 1019–1036.

Scheve, K. and Stasavage, D. (2010). The conscription of wealth: mass warfare and the demand for progressive taxation. *International Organization*, 64(4):529–561.

Scheve, K. and Stasavage, D. (2012). Democracy, war, and wealth: lessons from two centuries of inheritance taxation. *American Political Science Review*, 106(1):81–102.

Scott, A. and Storper, M. (2003). Regions, globalization, development. *Regional Studies*, 37(6–7):579–593.

Seligman, E. R. A. (1914). *The income tax: a study of the history, theory, and practice of income taxation at home and abroad.* The Lawbook Exchange, Ltd.

Shin, G.-W. (1998). Agrarian conflict and the origins of Korean capitalism. *American Journal of Sociology*, 103(5):1309–1351.

Soifer, H. D. (2013). State power and the economic origins of democracy. *Studies in Comparative International Development*, 48(1):1–22.

Soifer, H. D. (2015). *State building in Latin America*. Cambridge University Press.

Soifer, H. D. (2016). Regionalism, ethnic diversity, and variation in public good provision by national states. *Comparative Political Studies*, 49(10):1341–1371.

Soininen, A. M. (1974). *Old traditional agriculture in Finland in the 18th and 19th centuries. Agricultural and Food Science*, 46(Supplement). DOI: https://doi.org/10.23986/afsci.71864

Sokoloff, K. L. and Engerman, S. L. (2000). History lessons. *Journal of Economic Perspectives*, 14(3):217–232.

Solt, F. (2009). Standardizing the world income inequality database. *Social Science Quarterly*, 90(2):231–242.

Stasavage, D. (2005). Democracy and education spending in Africa. *American Journal of Political Science*, 49(2):343–358.

Stokes, S. C., Dunning, T., Nazareno, M., and Brusco, V. (2013). *Brokers, voters, and clientelism: the puzzle of distributive politics*. Cambridge University Press.

Stone, I. (1977). British direct and portfolio investment in Latin America before 1914. *The Journal of Economic History*, 37(3):690–722.

Suryanarayan, P. (2017). Hollowing out the state: franchise expansion and fiscal capacity in colonial India. Accessed at https://ssrn.com/abstract=2951947

Suryanarayan, P. and White, S. (2021). Slavery, reconstruction, and bureaucratic capacity in the American South. *American Political Science Review*, pages 1–17.

Tang, A. M. (1979). China's agricultural legacy. *Economic Development and Cultural Change*, 28(1):1–22.

Tilly, C. (1975). Reflections on the history of European state-making. *The formation of national states in Western Europe*, 38. Princeton University Press

Tilly, C. (1992). *Coercion, capital, and European states, AD 990–1992*. Blackwell Oxford.

Timmons, J. F. (2005). The fiscal contract: states, taxes, and public services. *World Politics*, 57(4):530–567.

UEA-CRU, Jones, P., Harris, I., et al. (2013). CRU TS3. 21: Climatic Research Unit (CRU) Time Series (TS) version 3.21 of high resolution gridded data of month-by-month variation in climate (Jan. 1901–Dec. 2012). NCAS British Atmospheric Data Centre.

Van Dijk, H., Foeken, D., and Van Til, K. (2001). Population mobility in Africa: an overview. In de Bruijn, M. E., Foeken, D. W. J., and van Dijk, R. A. (eds.),

Mobile Africa: changing patterns of movement in Africa and beyond, pages 9–26. Brill.

Venables, A. J. (2005). Spatial disparities in developing countries: cities, regions, and international trade. *Journal of Economic Geography*, 5(1):3–21.

Wheatcroft, S., Davies, R., and Cooper, J. (1986). Soviet industrialization reconsidered: some preliminary conclusions about economic development between 1926 and 1941. *Economic History Review*, 39(2): 264–294.

Wibbels, E. and Arce, M. (2003). Globalization, taxation, and burden-shifting in Latin America. *International Organization*, 57(1):111–136.

Williamson, J. G. (1965). Regional inequality and the process of national development: a description of the patterns. *Economic Development and Cultural Change*, 13(4, Part 2):1–84.

Willmott, C. and Matsuura, K. (2012). Terrestrial precipitation: 1900–2010 gridded monthly time series (v 3.02). Newark: Center for Climatic Research, Department of Geography, University of Delaware. http://climate.geog. udel.edu/~climate/html_pages/Global2011/Precip_revised_3.02/README .GlobalTsP2011.html

Wingender, A. (2014). Structural transformation in the 20th century: a new database on agricultural employment around the world. Technical report, Discussion Paper No. 14-28, Department of Economics, University of Copenhagen.

Acknowledgments

The authors thank Editor David Stasavage, David Rueda, Antonella Bandiera, Didac Queralt, Per Andersson, Adrián Lucardi, Florian Hollenbach, Jonathan Hanson, Vincent Mahler, Ryan Saylor, Ken Scheve, Rachel Sigman, Hillel Soifer, Ping Zhang, Xiaobo Lü, Scott Abramson, Mark Dincecco, Thiago Nascimento da Silva, Joe Grieco, Soomin Oh and participants in seminars at the Instituto Carlos III-Juan March, the State Capacity Workshop at Duke University, WPSA 2019, the Ludwig-Maximiliean Universität (Munich), the State Capacity Workshop at the Götesborg Universität, the Taxation and Fiscal Capacity Workshop at Peking University, ITAM, the SFB 884 Seminar Series at the Mannheim Universität, and the State Making and Global Order in Historical-Comparative Perspective at Lunds Universitet. We thank Glenn-Iain Steinback and Kristoffer Wikstrom for valuable research assistance.

Cambridge Elements ≡

Political Economy

David Stasavage

New York University

David Stasavage is Julius Silver Professor in the Wilf Family Department of Politics at New York University. He previously held positions at the London School of Economics and at Oxford University. His work has spanned a number of different fields and currently focuses on two areas: development of state institutions over the long run and the politics of inequality. He is a member of the American Academy of Arts and Sciences.

About the Series

The Element Series Political Economy provides authoritative contributions on important topics in the rapidly growing field of political economy. Elements are designed so as to provide broad and in-depth coverage combined with original insights from scholars in political science, economics, and economic history. Contributions are welcome on any topic within this field.

Cambridge Elements ☰

Political Economy

Elements in the Series

A full series listing is available at: www.cambridge.org/EPEC

Printed in the United States
by Baker & Taylor Publisher Services